HOW TO BE
CHIEF
EXECUTIVE
OF YOUR
OWN LIFE

HOW TO BE

CHIEF

EXECUTIVE

OF YOUR

OWN LIFE

MIKE WILSON

First published in 2018 by MSW

Copyright © Mike Wilson 2018

ISBN 978-1-911195-77-1

Typeset by Jill Sawyer Phypers
Cover design by Bosh Creative Services Ltd.
Printed and bound by
CPI Group (UK) Ltd, Croydon, CR0 4YY

This book is dedicated to

Sophie and my daughter, Panda, for their never-ending love, care and encouragement

and

Elizabeth Downie, my PA, and John Page, my driver for 39 years; the unbeatable back-up and support team

Proceeds from the sale of this book will go to the St. James's Place Charitable Foundation

'Mike has great charm and a quiet, modest charisma combined with empathy for everyone. He is greatly respected and loved by all, not for what he is, but who he is. This is what makes him stand out as a truly exceptional leader. He has mentored and coached many of our senior staff at Hope & Homes for Children – and it is of no surprise that we have dramatically improved our performance as a consequence. Soak up the learning so genuinely offered in this book. Apply it and anticipate success for yourself.'

Mark Cook, Founder, and Mark Waddington, CEO,
Hope & Homes for Children

'There has never, ever been an occasion, however bad things have seemed, when I have not finished a one-to-one with Mike feeling more fulfilled than when I started.'

Ben Backhouse, Founder, Risk Assured

'How many other CEOs have an investor whose first questions are always: "How is your daughter? Are you spending enough time with her? Are you prioritising what is important to you?" My daughter is only two years old. But as soon as she's old enough she will have her own copy of this book.'

Jennifer Sundberg and Pippa Begg,
co-CEOs, Board Intelligence

'It is hard to imagine that somebody who, along with his business partner of so many decades, built up a FTSE 100 company in his own lifetime . . . could remain so humble, kind and thoughtful. If they were to introduce a Nobel Prize for business, I feel certain that Mike should be the very first recipient.'

Joel Cadbury, Entrepreneur

CONTENTS

FOREWORD

by Mark Weinberg

MIKE'S WAY

MIKE WILSON AND I are credited with being the joint founders of the St. James's Place Wealth Management Group, which in 25 years has grown into a company managing funds of £75 billion and has become the second fastest company to qualify for the FTSE 100 Index.

The reality, though, is that while I must have made some contribution, principally on product design and presentation, the overwhelming driver of the Company's success has been that Mike, throughout that period, has managed its operations and motivated and inspired everyone who has worked for it.

How Mike arranged – and still arranges – his business and personal life is described in this book in his own words.

Sadly, I am not sufficiently self-disciplined to run my own life and to work in line with his guidance. In the book Mike frequently, with good humour, refers to my failings in these respects – arriving late for meetings, not remembering names of important members of the team and so on.

What I can say is that Mike runs his business life as meticulously as described in the book and even if you would, on reading the book, wonder whether you could follow his example, I am sure you will find his account inspirational and really helpful in the course of your business and, indeed, your personal life.

While I wholeheartedly recommend that everyone should read this book, I also want to use this opportunity to say a few things about Mike as a person – which he is far too modest to do himself. He is a brilliant leader of people, but perhaps more important than that, he is an extraordinary person himself. He makes everyone feel special and brings an element of excitement into even the most mundane business event. I don't think I know anyone who is as liked – and respected – as Mike is. I don't think one can underestimate to what extent those personal attributes have contributed to the success of the Company.

Over the years, and across the three companies in which I have had the pleasure of working with him, Mike has brought out the best in almost everyone whose world he has touched, however senior or junior. Even now that he has retired from an active leadership role, members of the SJP community and its financial advisers still look to him for inspiration, as well as receiving counselling from him.

It speaks to Mike's modesty that, initially, he thought there was no point in publishing this guide to how he runs his life. I convinced him that it offers people remarkable insights. He writes with clarity and the steps he recommends are simple to follow and could be adopted by anyone (with the possible exception of me!).

INTRODUCTION

A FEW YEARS AGO, I was flattered to be asked by a great friend and mentor, Dennis Stevenson (Lord Stevenson), to address an MBA course at Judge Business School in Cambridge.

The brief from Dennis was somewhat unusual: he told me to assume that I was on my deathbed with just 30 minutes to live and, during that time, I should give the members of the audience my top tips for them to have the best chance of leading successful and fulfilling lives.

This brief certainly applied my mind and presented me with the challenge of prioritising the tips I would pass on in such a short timescale.

The tips fell broadly under the chapter headings and sub-headings of this book, with the exception of Chapter 10, which covers the hidden benefits of charitable giving, something I have only come to appreciate more recently.

I should apologise at this stage because I often refer to writing various things down where most people would be tapping them into their computer. I do realise I'm a dinosaur!

I enjoyed giving the talk in Cambridge, which largely led to me deciding to write this book for three principle reasons:

Firstly, because of my frustration that there were so many more points I wanted to cover in my talk, but was unable to do so in the time allocated. In a sense, this book fleshes out what I would have said if Dennis had given me rather longer to live!

Secondly, because I have benefited so much from what I have learnt from Mark Weinberg, in particular, but also from the many other people whom I have had as mentors or who became role models for different aspects of my life. If just a few people could benefit from my experience, then I would be delighted.

And thirdly, I think most people, if they are honest, would like to leave some sort of legacy and I am no exception.

I once read that a legacy is: 'Leaving a lasting influence and is the sum of all outcomes from our behaviour that others continue to remember us by.'

This is more important to me than any financial legacy I may leave in my will – though my beneficiaries might disagree!

My choice of chapter headings such as 'You Can Choose Your Own Future' and 'Mind Over Matter' smack of 'management speak' and may put you off – but I hope not. I realise that these two chapter headings in particular could have come straight from the mouth of David Brent in *The Office*!

I am also conscious that the shelves of bookshops are already groaning with self-help books and that this could be seen as yet another one of those. But I hope not. The books that I have benefited from most have not been written by management gurus (although they are often very well-written) but are successful people's autobiographies, or are self-help books that are not just based on theory, but on the author's own practical experiences. I hope that this book will be a combination of these. At the end of each chapter there are key messages and there is also a pocket-sized pamphlet of key messages for use on the go.

The most important thing I have learnt is that, while we cannot change our past, we can choose our future; we are chief executives of our own lives. It was this realisation when I was aged 25 and joined Mark Weinberg at Abbey Life that was the turning point of my life and led to the title of this book.

I do assure you that this book is based solely on the practical experiences I have had – largely over the past 25 years at St. James's Place and the previous 23 years with Mark Weinberg at Hambro Life/Allied Dunbar. However, right at the beginning of the book, I want to give you a brief background to my life before then, which included very formative years for me and, in a very real sense, set me up for the many trials and tribulations that would follow.

CHAPTER 1

MY LIFE BEFORE
ST. JAMES'S PLACE

MY YOUNGER SISTER AND I were brought up in Bournemouth. My father was in the Royal Navy and I was fortunate enough to have a private education, partly funded by a naval bursary, at St. Edward's School, Oxford.

I had a wonderful, caring mother who devoted herself to my sister and I. In contrast, my father took little interest in either of us – unless we achieved success, when he felt proud of us.

My father worked at the Admiralty in London during most of my childhood and only came home to Bournemouth at weekends. He was a high achiever: he had gone to Dartmouth Royal Naval College and rose to become one of the youngest commanders in the Navy at the time. He had also been chief test pilot at Farnborough, for which he was awarded an Air Force Cross.

His passion was cars and much of his money and time were spent on them rather than on us, which meant we had no family holidays. He became a successful racing driver and competed each year at Le Mans in the 24-hour race, driving for Bristol Cars, which won the team prize on several occasions.

My father expected my sister and I to be successful at school – but gave us no encouragement. Unlike other parents, he would only turn up for school matches when we were selected for the 1st teams.

While I eventually got a place in the 1st XV rugby team and became captain of the swimming team, my academic career was less successful and my school reports did not fill my father with joy. I simply could not see the relevance of learning what had happened in 1066 and my mind during history classes was rather more preoccupied with how we could beat Marlborough College that afternoon at rugby. Unsurprisingly, I only scraped five O-levels (GCSEs) at age 16 and failed my A-levels two years later, much to my father's displeasure. This was despite having been offered a place at Oxford University because of my rugby if I just passed them, irrespective of grades.

Fortunately, my housemaster and the headmaster at St. Edward's never wrote me off completely and I became head of house for my last year at school. But this only slightly mollified my father.

My parents divorced during my last year at school and, subsequently, I only saw my father from time to time. While I was never close to him, despite his flaws he nevertheless did have a significant and positive influence on my life. My desire to be successful and my competitiveness certainly come from him – but I do hope that I emulate in some small way my mother's unselfishness and her attribute of caring for other people.

In my last term at school I had a meeting with the part-time careers master (he also taught me history). Unsurprisingly, he said my career options were somewhat limited. His only two suggestions were either I became a sports master, or applied to become a management trainee at the Rank Organisation. He only suggested Rank because he remembered an old boy of the school had been successful there and was now a director. I immediately opted for the latter because I associated Rank with the famous 'gong man' and J. Arthur Rank films, which I thought could perhaps lead to a glamorous career in the movies.

I quickly became disillusioned when I arrived in my very old, yellow, drop-head Morris Minor for the interview at – to my surprise – the depot of Rank Hovis McDougall, the bakery company. I did, however, accept their offer to become a management trainee. My career master's words about my career options being 'limited' were resounding in my ears.

For five months I worked on a bread delivery van, leaving the depot on the outskirts of Bournemouth at five each morning, which somewhat curtailed my social life. The only compensation was that I was allowed to consume one free doughnut a day.

I played squash each week after my bread round and my opponent on one occasion worked for the life assurance company Equity and Law (now AXA). On hearing how I was not enjoying my new-found career, he mentioned that Equity and Law in Bournemouth had a vacancy for a quotations clerk and suggested that I should apply. I did so, and was lucky enough to be accepted. They clearly missed my lack of qualifications for the role, having only passed O-level maths on my second sitting.

My Equity and Law career, on a starting salary of £350 per annum, involved preparing life policy quotations and doing a lot of photocopying for two very bossy secretaries.

After two years my manager saw that I was becoming restless and, for some reason, he thought I had some hidden potential as a salesman. He persuaded Head Office to allow me to become the company's youngest broker consultant (called inspector at the time). The role was to call on insurance brokers and bank managers who had agencies with Equity and Law to persuade them to sell our products to their clients or customers.

My success initially was limited – until I realised that perhaps the key was to persuade them to let me visit their clients or customers and effectively do the work for them. The bank managers in and around Bournemouth were very receptive to my proposal (not offered by other companies) and allowed me to contact those of their elderly customers who were potentially in the market to buy an annuity.

I would make three or four appointments a day, with mainly 70- to 80-year-olds, predominantly widows, who treated me as if I were their grandson, serving me cups of coffee and tea with cakes while I filled in the application forms before asking for their signature and cheque. Due to my relative success in this endeavour I was given the opportunity to move to Equity and Law's City office in London.

The bright lights of London appealed to me as a 23-year-old bachelor, but my damp basement bedsit in Fulham (hardly fashionable at the time) brought me down to earth. Equity and Law's salaries then were based on your age and not on your ability or how much business you secured for the company. My salary was by then £1,100 per annum, which didn't go far in London – although I must confess that I did some moonlighting as a model to top up my income, featuring in a cigarette commercial and also in an advertisement for the Milk Marketing Board as 'Pinta Man'!

Back to the day job. One of the most supportive insurance brokers I called on at Equity and Law was Charles Fry, who suggested on one occasion that we should meet up over the weekend with our girlfriends for dinner. Much to my embarrassment, I had to explain to him that I didn't 'do dinners' and that my budget only stretched to the occasional evening out at the Loose Box wine bar in Knightsbridge. This led to a discussion about what I was being paid at the time. Upon hearing, Charles immediately said that he would get me an interview at a company called Abbey Life, founded by Mark Weinberg, who was revolutionising the life assurance market. He said Mark was not interested in age or qualifications – clearly a big plus from my point of view – he was only interested in results, and paid accordingly.

I joined Abbey Life aged 25 in 1968. It proved to be the turning point of my career. My life changed beyond all recognition. This was the start, albeit at a very junior level at the time, of a 50-year working association with Mark.

Abbey Life was a meritocracy where you stood or fell on your results which, while somewhat frightening at times, appealed to my competitive nature.

After a year I was promoted to City broker manager and, two years later, to London area manager. Life was good. I could now afford not only drinks at the Loose Box, but dinner afterwards. I bought a flat in South Kensington and my chosen company car was a Lotus 2+2 (because of its looks) although I did have to pay my flatmate to start it most mornings – it was highly temperamental.

The 'good life' I was enjoying started to seem rather precarious when Mark Weinberg and the board of Abbey Life suddenly resigned following a fallout with Abbey's parent company, ITT, in 1970.

Mark, having founded Abbey Life, however, decided he wanted to create another life assurance company and, with both the backing and name of Hambros Bank, Hambro Life was launched in 1971. I jumped at the opportunity to become a day-one employee of the new venture.

Mark's stated aim was for Hambro Life to become quoted on the stock exchange after only five years. This was duly achieved in 1976. I was appointed to the board as sales and marketing director – at the age of 33.

Two members of the board were Joel Joffe (the late Lord

Joffe) and Sir Sydney Lipworth, who were both inspirational and who, together with Dennis Stevenson, an adviser to the company, and Mark had a massive influence on my career and life. When I became a director, all the other members of the Hambro Life board had their many qualifications and degrees shown after their name in the company's report and accounts, as well as in the marketing literature. Mark, sensitive to my own lack of qualifications, changed this practice going forward to save me embarrassment.

One day in 1988 Mark said, without warning, that he wished to step down as chief executive and become chairman. He offered me the role of chief executive. I quickly responded that, while I was very flattered, I loved being the sales director – and declined the offer. As he walked out of my office he turned and asked me to let him know over the next day or so which of my colleagues I would like to be reporting to as the new chief executive. Five minutes later, I went to Mark's office and said that I had changed my mind and would accept the role.

British American Tobacco (BAT), a conglomerate, had acquired Hambro Life (which had been renamed Allied Dunbar) in 1985 for £660 million, with the usual promises that they would allow us to retain our autonomy. In 1989 I joined the board of BAT, which entitled me to a free allocation of cigarettes each month.

It was not long, however, before BAT was itself subject to a hostile takeover bid from a consortium called Hoylake headed by Jimmy Goldsmith, Kerry Packer and Jacob Rothschild (Lord Rothschild). The bid failed in the end, but BAT was urged by the City and its shareholders to cease being a diversified group and to become more focused. Its various subsidiaries were disposed of – such as Wiggins Teape, Argos and Saks Fifth Avenue. It decided to focus, unsurprisingly, on tobacco – but also on financial services where it owned an insurance company in America called Farmers, as well as Eagle Star and us in the UK.

This 'increased focus' did not sit well with Mark, myself and the Allied Dunbar management team and – following BAT's rejection of an offer from Barclays Bank to acquire 51% of Allied Dunbar and for us to market financial services to their customers – I resigned.

Mark had already resigned from BAT's board and was on Jacob Rothschild's board and so knew him well. Jacob had always predicted that Mark and I would not enjoy life working for a subsidiary of BAT, or indeed of any company, and had offered us his backing to form a new financial services company once we eventually realised his prediction was correct.

The opportunity to start again from scratch with Mark, backed by Jacob, was appealing, but at the same time nerve-racking. However, I realised that I never wanted to reach retirement thinking 'I wonder if . . .'.

Following an excellent and most enjoyable dinner at Mosimann's, Mark and I shook hands on our partnership as joint founders of J. Rothschild Assurance (JRA). We agreed to launch the new company in a year's time, and this was the start of the most enjoyable and fulfilling years of my life.

The first three months were the honeymoon period as we bounced numerous ideas around. These were captured on flip chart sheets or on the back of envelopes in Mark's multi-coloured scribbles.

Reality then hit: we had to have an action plan and make some final decisions in order to launch nine months later.

The split of the various tasks that needed completing fell very naturally between Mark and myself; we didn't have job descriptions but played to our very different, individual strengths. There were many late nights (Mark doesn't do early mornings), and Sunday afternoons always involved a lengthy catch-up on the phone and agreeing a plan for the week ahead.

The Company was launched in January 1992 with Mark as Chairman and me as Chief Executive.

BAT portrayed us as little more than a cottage industry – not to be taken seriously or viewed as a competitor. This was music to our ears and spurred us on to prove them wrong.

In 1997, JRA became a publicly quoted company as St. James's Place (SJP).

In 2016, SJP joined the FTSE 100.

On **1st January 2017**, on the **25th anniversary** of St. James's Place, its market capitalisation exceeded **£5 billion**, with funds under management totalling **£75 billion**.

CHAPTER 2

YOU CAN CHOOSE YOUR OWN FUTURE

You can't change your past – you can change your future

I HOPE THAT EVERYONE who reads this book will find areas that are relevant and important to them. Not everything will strike a chord immediately – much will depend on where you are in your life and in your career right now. This chapter, however, will hopefully speak to all of you, wherever you are and whatever you're doing.

If I had to boil it down to one, succinct message, it would be this: you should – and can – be in control of your life and to get to this state you need to create a vision of what you want your life to be, and constantly measure yourself against it. The same is true for a company as it is for an individual.

Friends have told me that this chapter goes on for too long. They may have a point! But, to my mind, it is the key to everything that follows – both in this book and in life. For those of you who don't have the time right now to read every word, there is a summary at the end of the chapter.

PERSONAL VISION AND GOALS

I was 33 when I first created a vision for myself. Over the years it has changed, inevitably – my dreams no longer involve sports cars! – but I have never lost sight of the importance of having that vision.

To go forward, we need to forget about who we were and to focus on who we can be. All of us will have regrets about what we have or have not done in the past, but that's history. You cannot change what's already happened.

What you can do is to choose your future and achieve what you want in life if you remember that you are chief executive of your own life.

You may not have that title on your visiting card – but that's what you are.

Why do I say that?

It is the chief executive of a company who has the ultimate responsibility for the company's vision, and who sets the goals and focuses on attaining them. The chief executive has the most control and influence over the future of his or her company.

In the same way, no single individual has more influence over your future than you. Who other than you should set the goals for your life and be responsible for achieving them?

You should appreciate that:

❏   **you** are the best asset that you can ever invest in

❏   **you**, personally, are the major investor in your life and your future, and how you invest in your own personal development is your choice

❏ **you** may well be a shrewd investor in assets such as shares, but how the companies you have selected actually perform in practice is not within your control. That is down to other people.

Contrast that last point with the investment you make in yourself; you are the asset that you can exercise most control over and how you perform is down to you and not to other people.

To stretch the metaphor even further, your investment in developing yourself offers you the greatest potential return as well as the opportunity of personal fulfilment. If you buy into these two fundamental points you will appreciate that it's important to take responsibility for your life in order to control your own future.

CREATING A VISION

Creating your own vision for the future is the easy bit, but a vision alone won't determine your future. The best vision, the most inspiring goals and smartest strategy in the world are totally meaningless unless you act on them.

Nelson Mandela once said:

> *'Vision without action is only a dream. Action without vision is only a way of passing time. Vision with action can change the world.'*

President Kennedy in 1960 provided NASA with a very clear vision:

> *'We will put a man on the moon by the*
> *end of the decade.'*

❏ It was brief.

❏ It was specific.

❏ It had a timescale.

❏ It was ambitious.

❏ It was challenging.

Kennedy realised that (in the words of Abraham Lincoln): 'The best way to predict your future is to create it.' But Kennedy's vision wouldn't have been achieved without an action plan incorporating clear goals – or stepping stones – along the way.

In the same way that President Kennedy had a vision for his country, business leaders should have a vision for their companies.

Mark's and my vision for J. Rothschild Assurance (the company changed its name to St. James's Place in 2000) was very clear and precise (as you will see later). The headline vision was:

> *'A stock market quote for J. Rothschild Assurance*
> *five years from launch.'*

Again, it was specific, had a timescale and was ambitious and challenging.

A vision for one's country (in the case of Kennedy) – or one's company in the case of driven and ambitious business leaders – will often be the dominant factor in personal visions also.

But a word of warning: a personal vision should not be limited to your working life. You should have a mental picture of what your perfect future will or could be like – your *Perfect Life* – and that should include **all** aspects of your life.

I lost sight of this when I first created a vision for myself. I had recently become sales director of Hambro Life aged 33. Mark, through our weekly one-to-one meetings converted me from only thinking as a salesman and focusing almost exclusively on the volume of sales, to thinking as a businessman and focusing on profits.

Mark suggested that I should find an outside coach for my own personal development. I was recommended an American lady called Jinny Ditzler, who successfully persuaded me that I should take responsibility for my own life, and of the importance of goals and of having a vision.

The combination of Mark and Jinny transformed my business life – although it was a very steep learning curve. It also brought home to me the value of having not just one coach or mentor, who is unlikely to be able to help with both business expertise and personal development.

Jinny's very clear advice was that I should develop goals and a vision for **all** aspects of my life (not just business), which I duly did and put down on a sheet of paper. This might be booking family holidays at the start of the year, playing tennis once a week to keep fit, and so on.

However, despite her best endeavours, Jinny failed over two years of regular meetings to get me to focus on anything other than my working life. I merely paid lip service to everything else, writing the goals down as instructed, and then failing to act on them. I hasten to add that this isn't a criticism of Jinny – but of me. I was convinced at the time that success in business was everything.

Jinny's support enabled me to achieve what I so desperately wanted in my business life. Although, unsurprisingly, my life overall was far from being perfect! I was working 60 hours a week, going into the office on Sunday afternoons and doing three business dinners a week. I had little or no time for any personal life.

I confess that it was only when I was in my mid-50s that I appreciated that I needed to reassess my goals in life and to develop a fresh vision for my future. This time I was determined that it would include **all** aspects of my life.

My change of heart was triggered by the death of a close friend.

The person who was going to give the address at my friend's memorial service came to see me. He wanted my advice on the positive aspects of this friend's life that I felt he should include in his address. I really struggled with this and I could only come up with my friend's great sense of humour and success in business – which everyone already knew about. So I was not very helpful.

Reflecting on this brought home to me that my life was hardly different. I needed to make my life more rounded and more fulfilling (and not just in order to give people something to talk about after I was gone!).

Are you happy with what a close friend would be able to say about you and the different aspects of your life were you to die tomorrow?

PERSONAL AUDIT

I decided that the logical starting point was to carry out an **audit** on all the key aspects of my current life. I jotted these down on a sheet of paper under headings such as:

Business/work

Financial situation

Family relationships

Social life/holidays

Outside interests/hobbies

Voluntary work/charity

Health/physical fitness

Work/life balance

To demonstrate the value of carrying out your own personal audit, here's a snapshot of my life when I was aged 54. I am certainly not proud of it!

My **business life/work** was going really well. I was Chief Executive of St. James's Place, we'd gone public and my **financial situation** was healthy.

However, I was paying a high price for this.

My 60-hour working week, going to the office on Sunday afternoons and three business dinners a week meant that, for the majority of the time, I was an absent husband – and an absent father to Panda, my daughter. Throughout her childhood, on weekdays I left home before she got up and returned after she had gone to bed. I'm ashamed to say that school sports days and speech days never featured in my diary. The same pattern continued long after she left school. It was hardly surprising that I had not built a close **relationship** with my daughter – and she was already 23. This really hit home to me and is something I will always regret because no amount of money will buy back the past.

My **social life**, as a consequence of my work schedule, was virtually non-existent and I never took my full **holiday** entitlement. I deluded myself that the overseas business conventions I attended each year in wonderful venues and luxury hotels were holidays.

My **interests and hobbies** also scored a blank.

My involvement with **charities** was limited to making occasional reactive donations.

My **health/physical fitness** was standing up well (much to my doctor's surprise) – despite my smoking and lack of regular exercise. I knew, however, that it would take its toll eventually if I didn't change things.

I hardly need to comment on my **work/life balance** – it was extremely lopsided.

This audit of my life 20 years ago did provide me with a sharp reality check at the time. The positive was that I was starting from a low base and I could envisage taking steps to improve my situation. It spurred me on to create a mental picture of what I would want a similar personal audit to reflect five years on.

I spent a considerable amount of time visualising how I would feel and what it would mean to me for my vision to be reality rather than just a dream.

The audit forced me to take Jinny Ditzler's advice from some 20 years earlier and, this time, to include **all** aspects of life.

My life since the audit has changed beyond all recognition and is far more fulfilling – partly because of the contrast with my previous way of life. My grandchildren still call me 'Grandpa Puff Puff'; as although I'm now only on electronic cigarettes the name has stayed. 'Grandpa **Electronic** Puff Puff' would be a bit of a mouthful and not a great improvement!

It also bears mentioning that, by balancing my work/life scales – which were pretty much grounded at one end before – my work has not suffered in any way. The last 20 years have, if anything, been the most successful of my career.

Importantly, I now appreciate that the four most fulfilling aspects of my life are:

❏ having choice

❏ making a difference

❏ memories

❏ relationships.

Having Choice
I have always enjoyed making money and still do. My only regret is that it took me so long to appreciate that the real value of money was to give me **choice** in life. This didn't mean necessarily spending it on material things (or so-called status symbols). However, I did realise that I had more credibility if people knew that, while I could actually afford to have, say, a Bentley or a villa in Barbados, I had chosen not to.

Making a Difference
The most rewarding opportunity money gave me was to **make a difference** to the lives of others – whether they were family or close friends in need of financial help for, say, medical treatment, or towards a deposit for a flat as a first step to getting on the housing ladder.

I was also able to give money to the beneficiaries in my will at a time when they needed money the most, rather than the timing being dependent on when I die. I subscribe to the view that it's more fulfilling to give with a warm hand rather than a cold one.

Just as importantly, it enabled me to make charitable donations to make a difference to those less fortunate than myself.

Memories
What money does give me is the choice to facilitate events or family holidays which create lasting **memories**, such as Christmas in Antigua. However, I have many other wonderful memories which didn't cost money, such as watching my grandchildren swimming the length of a pool for the first time or appearing in their school play.

Relationships
The one thing money certainly cannot buy is **relationships**. These are built by spending time with people, enjoying, respecting, valuing and caring for them. This applies to all relationships whether with family, friends or work colleagues. Sophie, my partner, and I spend a lot of time together just in our own company. For many of our holidays we go on our own (often to the surprise of many people) because we do actually enjoy each other's company.

I have enormous love and respect for So͜
continual support and care, which I endeavou.

PERSONAL GOALS

One of the most enjoyable aspects of my present role at St. James's Place, since recently stepping down as Chairman, is giving one-to-one coaching to several of our financial advisers. They range from those who are already highly successful to those aspiring to be so. An individual can often swing from profound insecurity to massive overconfidence – particularly in the case of high flyers.

My main objective is to encourage them to make the most of their lives, to learn from the mistakes I and they have made, and not to take as long as I did to achieve their own *Perfect Life*.

The majority of people I speak to have given no thought to what their future could be like; many have no specific goals other than their production target for the following year. The only goal one successful adviser had was to buy the latest Ferrari in three years' time. He achieved his goal – but his joy was short-lived when an investment banker client of his bought a more up-to-date model three months later!

Others, usually only when prompted, do have in their minds a vision of their lives in, say, 10 years' time or at retirement, which is a good starting point. What they have given little or no thought to is **how** they are going to achieve it.

My challenge is to persuade everyone not just to have a vision for their future covering **all** aspects of their lives, but to convince them that they will only achieve this by setting personal goals to which they are 100% committed.

Having a vision of what my future would or could be like

was invaluable to me. However, without my commitment to short-term personal goals, my life would not have turned out the way it has today. I would never have had the outcome to which I aspired.

I say short-term goals because they provide the important sense of urgency. I believe there's a natural tendency in all of us to put things off.

Goals should form an essential part of your strategy to achieve the end game. They are the stepping stones on the way and they keep you on track.

Arriving at your personal goals is the easy bit; the challenge is having an ongoing commitment to them. How many people make New Year's resolutions that never come to anything? Were their resolutions just wishful thinking – or were they real commitments?

One thing in particular that has worked for me is cementing in my commitment to my goals by continually trying to visualise how I will feel and what it will mean to me to hit a particular goal.

PERSONAL OBSTACLES AND HURDLES

Anticipate the inevitable.

Obstacles and hurdles will be in our way and we run the danger of them knocking us off track as we strive to achieve our goals. Some will be real, others poor excuses.

'I didn't achieve my goals last year because I had a useless manager who didn't motivate me' – has often been said to me by a St. James's Place adviser in their first one-to-one session with me. It's a poor excuse.

I tactfully make the point that an effective manager should be viewed as a welcome bonus and not a requirement for the adviser to achieve personal success. I then go on to ask whether or not they want to be in control of their own destiny as far as possible, rather than to rely on others.

It's clearly essential that we work out how to overcome real obstacles to achieving our goals, which is often not easy – however, as I said earlier, the strength of an individual (or company) is their resilience and their ability to bounce back from adversity.

Those that achieve this do so because of their burning desire to succeed. They are totally focused and committed to achieving their goals come what may. Nothing will stop them.

'A winner is a dreamer who never gives up.'

Nelson Mandela

There's a saying that: 'Obsession doesn't guarantee success but lack of obsession does guarantee failure.'

PERSONAL VISUALISATION

'Power of visualisation – we think in pictures way more than we think in words.'

Nick Faldo

Visualisation of a future event is a very powerful tool that I first discovered when I was 17 years old. My burning desire and goal was not to do well in my exams (and I didn't) – but to be selected for my school's 1st XV rugby team. I envisaged how I would feel seeing my name for the first time on the

1st XV team sheet, telling my parents and running onto the pitch for my first match in front of the whole school.

I might have got my priorities wrong – but it worked for me. When it actually happened, I felt elated. I'm convinced that having visualised how I would feel played a big part in being selected for the 1st XV.

Here's another example of the power of visualisation:

One of the goals of one St. James's Place adviser was to achieve Partner level of production for the year for the first time.

At our regular one-to-one meetings I encouraged him to envisage what it would actually mean to him. How he would feel on the day when it was announced at our Company's Annual Meeting in January? This would be in front of five thousand people when he would receive the recognition for which he was striving.

❏ His name would be listed in the programme.

❏ His name would flash up on the screen as a first-time Partner qualifier.

❏ He would receive gold cufflinks for his achievement at a special reception before dinner.

I asked him to imagine how he would feel walking down the steps into the ballroom at the Grosvenor House Hotel for the Annual Partner Dinner and receiving a standing ovation from his peers and all the attendees.

I'm certainly not claiming the credit, but he did achieve his goal and may well have done so without my encouragement. But he was kind enough to say that once he'd visualised how he would feel, he knew that nothing was going to stop him.

His only regret was that he hadn't committed himself to this goal earlier because he had never been on such a high as on that day.

An article on Steve Backley, the javelin thrower and medal winner at three different Olympic Games, recounted how he had surgery on his Achilles tendon only 10 weeks before the Games in Atlanta in 1996. He was unable to train physically and said:

> *'I did all my prep in my head – it was invaluable*
> *for the rest of my career because I realised what*
> *the mind can do. The main skill I brushed up on*
> *was the ability to visualise and see what the future*
> *might hold. Once you have mastered this you can*
> *almost pre-empt the future.'*

You won't be surprised to learn that I firmly believe Steve Backley is right. The power of visualisation is extraordinarily potent.

SECRETS TO SUCCESS

Sadly they don't exist.

But what you can do is to plan to be successful and then give yourself the very best chance of success and of hitting your goals. This is achieved by giving it 100% – you can't do more than that.

Don't beat yourself up if you fail to reach your goals – the positive is that you will have certainly improved the key aspects of your life from the starting point shown in your original personal audit.

Let's take two examples:

1. Assume your **financial position** five years ago showed you had total borrowings of £300,000. Your goal was to reduce this to nil by today. You have given it your best shot and you've succeeded in reducing your borrowings to £60,000.

   You haven't achieved your goal but you have reduced your borrowings by 80%.

2. Five years ago, your personal audit showed a blank under, say, **health/physical fitness**. You decided to take up golf and your goal was to have a handicap of 12 within five years. You have achieved a handicap of 15. You have stuck to your objectives of having a lesson and playing golf on average once a week. You have been committed to achieving your goal and given it 100% over the five years.

   You haven't achieved your goal but you are physically fitter and you have progressed to having a golf handicap of 15 in only five years.

   While in neither case have you achieved your highly ambitious goals, you have every right to celebrate.

IT'S SIMPLE – NOT EASY

I hope you will agree that everything covered so far is fairly straightforward – simple – but it would be a mistake to think that because it's simple, it's easy. Because it most definitely is not!

I read that most people go through life operating at under 20% of their true potential. Do you want to be one of them?

Do you want to reach retirement facing disappointment because you didn't visualise the quality of life you wanted in retirement and the income required to fund it?

And/or be one of the many people who retire asking themselves: 'I wonder if I could have achieved this or that?'

Or who say: 'I feel I was capable of achieving more.'

The reason they feel this way is because they know that they never realised their full potential and that they will never know what they could have achieved or were actually capable of.

They didn't have a personal vision and a commitment to realistic – but stretching – goals to achieve it.

Success in achieving your vision or goals will, however, depend 20% on your strategy and plan and 80% on the delivery or execution. This is similar to companies; the business plan is the simple bit. Delivery and execution is the real challenge for individuals and companies.

COMPANY VISION AND GOALS

The importance for individuals of having a vision, goals, anticipating hurdles and the value of visualisation applies equally strongly to companies. While the visions will be different – companies rarely play squash! – the process is broadly similar.

The original vision for J. Rothschild Assurance – and the steps we took to achieve it.

Mark and I had made the decision in late 1990 to leave Allied Dunbar (previously called Hambro Life) which had been taken over by BAT in 1985.

Jacob Rothschild had offered to back us (together with Scottish Amicable) to start a new financial services company and J. Rothschild Assurance (JRA) was launched in January 1992.

Our vision for the Company was very clear and precise:

> *'A stock market quote for J. Rothschild Assurance –*
> *five years from launch.'*

In 1997 (five years later) our vision became reality when JRA became a quoted company.

While a stock market quote after five years was our headline vision, our vision also included the following, which have also been achieved:

❑ For the Company to remain independently managed.

❑ For the Partnership to become the most professional and trusted adviser of financial advice in the UK.

❑ To create from day one the J. Rothschild Assurance Foundation, a charitable foundation supported by our people to give back to those less fortunate than ourselves.

We wanted that last aim to be embedded in our company culture.

I should make it clear that I, personally, had very little say in the timing of our vision for JRA to be a quoted company after only five years – it was non-negotiable. Mark had founded our previous company (Hambro Life) and had achieved just that.

We had to go public with our very challenging vision to attract the exceptional team required for the Company to succeed.

JRA was going to stand or fall on its ability to build its own team of high-quality, experienced and successful financial advisers in order to distribute its products and services. These potential recruits had considerable financial incentives to remain with their existing companies. The same applied to the majority of senior employees we wished to take on.

When Mark and I left Allied Dunbar to launch JRA we knew BAT/Allied Dunbar – initially our main target for recruits – would put the financial case for why their people should not join us. Their tactic played on the short-term financial logic for their people to stay. Our tactic was to play on the potential longer-term financial benefits our opportunity offered, enabling them to make **personal capital** through founder shares and building their practices.

But, very importantly, we appealed to their **emotions** – highlighting the excitement of being a pioneer and the pride their children and grandchildren would have in being able to say: 'My father or mother was a founder member of J. Rothschild Assurance.'

We persuaded the joiners that they would be working with people they knew and trusted and that our new venture with the Rothschild name would revitalise them. Of course, our tactic did not work with all of them but fortunately it did with many.

Our Audit of the Competition
We analysed the features of all of our competitors and what they offered both their advisers and clients. This was particularly important in respect of Allied Dunbar, our previous company and a major source of potential recruits for us. The results of this exercise, starting with a clean sheet of paper, enabled us to arrive at what we felt were **the 10 key**

attributes for J. Rothschild Assurance to succeed in an already overcrowded marketplace.

With tongue firmly in cheek, we called this:

Utopia Life

It formed the heart of our recruitment proposition during the first five years of JRA.

Utopia Life

The 10 key attributes for J. Rothschild Assurance to succeed:

1. Our own team of experienced, high-quality advisers.

2. High productivity and a high retention rate of advisers whose own interests were aligned with JRA.

3. Building personal capital for the future through both the Partners' Capital Plan and having an equity interest in JRA.

4. Our target market was the higher/high net worth market.

5. We needed to offer a wide and competitive range of products and services.

6. We would strive for excellent service and a distinctive approach to investment management.

7. **JRA needed financial strength.**

8. **An experienced (and innovative) board and management team.**

9. **An excellent brand and reputation.**

10. **The right corporate culture to succeed.**

Our Company Goals

Our ambitious timeline led us to get advice very early on from the corporate advice team at Barclays de Zoete Wedd (BZW). We wanted a clear idea of what JRA needed to achieve and the shape in which the business had to be in order to obtain a public quote.

Based on this advice we developed key performance indicators for the first five years for:

❏ new business

❏ growth in the size of the Partnership (our financial advisers)

❏ average productivity per Partner

❏ the increase, retention and amount of funds under management.

We knew that achieving these goals each year would build a profitable business which would enable us to achieve our vision.

Obstacles and Hurdles
As with any business, unforeseen obstacles and hurdles were put in our way during those early years:

❑ a poor economy

❑ a weak stock market

❑ a massive increase in regulation.

We overcame these temporary setbacks because the key executives were 100% focused and obsessive about delivering our five-year goal.

The ownership of the vision didn't just rest with Mark and me. It was spread as widely as possible among the senior management team who were motivated by their overwhelming desire not to let down the early joiners (founder members) of the Company – far more so than by their own potential financial gain.

Summary: Our Visualisation for J. Rothschild Assurance
Visualisation of how we would feel played a major part in enabling us to achieve our vision of becoming a publicly quoted company. We visualised:

❑ the delight of delivering on the promise to those early joiners

❑ the press headlines

❑ seeing the JRA share price in the *Financial Times*

and last, but not least:

❏ the pleasure we'd have in proving wrong the cynics who, when we launched, portrayed JRA as no more than a cottage industry – not to be taken seriously or viewed as a competitor!

The steps we took in order to achieve our vision for J. Rothschild Assurance were:

❏ creating a vision for the Company in the first place

❏ carrying out an audit (of our competitors)

❏ having goals

❏ anticipating the inevitable obstacles and hurdles

I think you will agree that these steps to achieve the vision for J. Rothschild Assurance are very similar to the steps recommended earlier for individuals to achieve their personal visions.

*Remember, there are no secrets to success; the steps
to take are simple but not easy.*

KEY MESSAGES

YOU CAN CHOOSE YOUR OWN FUTURE
You can't change your past – you can choose your future

- **You are chief executive of your own life**
- **You are the best asset that you can ever invest in**
  - ➪ invest in your own personal development
- **Conduct a personal audit of all key aspects of your life today:**
  - ➪ business/work
  - ➪ financial situation
  - ➪ family relationships
  - ➪ social life/holidays
  - ➪ outside interests/hobbies
  - ➪ voluntary work/charity
  - ➪ health/physical fitness
  - ➪ work/life balance
- **Create your own vision for all the key aspects of your life in five years' time**
- **Fulfilment in life:**
  - ➪ having choice
  - ➪ making a difference
  - ➪ memories
  - ➪ relationships
- **Set goals, stepping stones, to achieve your five-year vision**
  - ➪ 80% will be down to delivery or execution

- **100% commitment to your goals**
  - ➪ visualise how you will feel and what it will mean to you to hit a particular goal
  - ➪ have key objectives each month to ensure you stay on track
- **Realise your full potential**
  - ➪ Don't retire asking yourself, 'I wonder if . . .?'
- **The challenges and steps for a company to achieve its vision**

CHAPTER 3

MIND OVER MATTER

Your attitude will determine your future

THE NUMEROUS HEALTH CLUBS, gyms, keep-fit books, DVDs and personal trainers show the very large number of people who acknowledge the importance of physical fitness to keep their bodies in good shape.

Our minds are far more complex than our bodies and standard training programmes for the mind don't exist.

Far less choice is available to keep our minds in good shape and functioning effectively, despite the fact that success in business – or indeed in any walk of life – is often dependent on having the right mindset. It's therefore very much down to us to learn to manage our minds and to develop the right attitude. Although the demands of sport are largely physical, psychological support is now acknowledged as being of great importance. In this respect, anyway, sport is ahead of business.

Being in peak physical condition and having the right mental attitude are two key attributes of top sports people. A good example is Novak Djokovic, one of the all-time greatest tennis players. While he is superbly fit, as are all top players, Simon Briggs in the *Daily Telegraph* described him as 'a uniquely disciplined character'. Djokovic dedicates 15 minutes a day to mind exercises – and if a match seems to be going against him, he has the remarkable ability to *reboot himself and come back for the next point.* Andy Murray has also shown he has that same ability.

The attitude of most people is that they are powerless to control their future and just accept that what will be, will be. In contrast, those who have self-discipline and willpower try to control their own future and, like Djokovic and Murray, have the ability to reboot themselves to come back when, inevitably, things get tough or go wrong. They firmly believe in the power of **mind over matter**, and value the ability to master themselves far more than any academic qualifications they may have.

On joining Mark Weinberg's life assurance company, Abbey Life, at age 25, it hit me that many people there had more academic qualifications and natural ability than me. After much soul-searching, I realised that any success I was to have in my career would have to depend on four key factors:

❏ my attitude – how I regarded things and reacted to events

❏ my self-discipline

❏ my willpower

❏ my resilience.

None of these could be tested in a classroom by way of a written exam at a set point in time. They would be tested in the real world, every day throughout my life, and I could see the benefit of focusing on them.

My motivation was very simple. I thought that since, whether I liked it or not, the majority of my waking life for the foreseeable future was going to be spent working, then I might as well try to be as successful as I could be at it. If I wanted to avoid looking back on my life thinking, 'I wonder if I could have achieved this or that', I should try to realise my full potential and hopefully reap any financial benefits that followed.

I had always liked sport at school. I quickly transferred my competitive spirit on the sports field to the workplace, where I also wanted to win both as an individual and, more importantly, for my company to be a winner. I was only too aware that the opposite of winning is losing – in the same way that I realised that the opposite to success was failure.

My passion for winning and success is largely driven by my fear of losing and failure. I often feel insecure and have self-doubts, but I don't view this as a weakness because security can lead to complacency. My insecurity makes me try harder and it ensures that I don't take things for granted. I often pinch myself and think how fortunate I am.

To win in life you should never stop learning, not only from your own successes and failures but from the successes and failures of others.

I have always believed that I would get nearer to achieving excellence if I strove for perfection. I've always striven to improve my performance in my particular role at the time – whether as a clerk, salesman, manager, sales director, chief executive, chairman or, today, as president.

I know that if I ever feel that I cannot continue to learn and improve and find myself thinking I've arrived then I'm actually past it and should call it a day.

> *It's often said that a company either grows or it dies – this applies equally to an individual.*

You learn more when things are tough than when things are going well.

'Tough times don't last. Tough people do.'

Floyd Mayweather

The strength of an individual or company lies in their resilience and their ability to deal with setbacks and to reboot themselves in order to bounce back from adversity. Failure isn't falling down – it's staying down. In the words of the great **Nelson Mandela**:

'Do not judge me by my successes; judge me by how many times I fell down and got back up again.'

Life – like the stock market – is volatile and it wouldn't be enjoyable if we didn't experience the inevitable lows as well as the highs. The lows test us and are necessary to appreciate fully the highs – the failures make the successes that much sweeter.

Your attitude determines your reaction to events and I try wherever possible to be **half full** rather than half empty. **Optimism** is one of the key characteristics of resilient people. Whenever I feel down I remind myself how many people are in a worse position than me.

When I was diagnosed with lung cancer at the age of 71 – having had prostate cancer 10 years earlier – the first thing I did was to write down the numerous positives in my life to weigh up against the only real negative at the time. I felt this would put my life into perspective and I reminded myself to do so every day by looking at my list.

MIKE WILSON: UPDATED AUDIT
(September 2014)

ONLY NEGATIVE
Having lung cancer.

NUMEROUS POSITIVES
- ✓ It's me with cancer (at age 71) and **not**, for example, Sophie, Panda, Oli, Marc or our grandchildren who are all healthy (remember Steve Sutton died of cancer in his 20s).
- ✓ I'm still alive – 10 years after having prostate cancer.
- ✓ I'm not in pain.
- ✓ I'm fine mentally – I'd rather have a physical illness than a mental one.
- ✓ No one could show me more love or support than Sophie and Panda.
- ✓ I have a wonderful support team of family, friends (Dennis), people at SJP
  - Elizabeth and John in particular.
- ✓ My financial situation enables me to:
  - Afford the best medical treatment available
  - Live in comfort and enjoy great holidays anywhere in the world
  - Know that Sophie, Panda and my grandchildren will be adequately provided for.
- ✓ I don't have a long bucket list of things I haven't done or want to do.

✓ I now appreciate in life many things I previously
took for granted.

✓ When I die I will leave a legacy:
- SJP and its culture
- SJP Foundation and my Charitable Trust
- CBE – external recognition.

✓ I've enjoyed a great life and travelled the world.
My life compared to 99%+ of the world's
population has been fantastic. I'm one of the very
few lucky ones!
- Meeting Sophie 18 years ago transformed my
personal life and happiness.
- Joining Mark Weinberg (Joel and Syd) when I
was 25 transformed my working life.
- My working life has enabled me to help to
create a successful company and transform the
lives of many.

When aspects of St. James's Place have gone wrong I
have always reminded myself of what has gone well for the
Company. I console myself by thinking that we must be doing
more things right than wrong to have achieved what we have
to date. I then look at the positives and remind myself that:

❑ we can learn from our mistakes, be a better company and
ensure that we don't make the same mistake again

❑ this is a real opportunity for the leadership team to prove
their worth and give added value.

When things are going really well it's often down to a favourable environment and the momentum of the business rather than the top team. Many senior executives, myself included, have benefited from this – in the form of pay rises and bonuses – as the remuneration committees of many quoted companies merely respond to the figures rather than carrying out an analysis of exactly what is driving the success.

We have all come across people from time to time who say they are feeling depressed because a specific event has occurred in their life or their financial circumstances resulting in them losing many friends. I am always quick to remind them that this is not actually a negative and that it's a positive that they now know who their genuine friends are as opposed to acquaintances or hangers-on from the past. It's important to have the right mindset.

I constantly remind myself that, so often, good will come from adversity – although it may be far from obvious at the time.

Do you have the ability to respond in the right way to failure?

Do you have the self-discipline, willpower and resilience to meet challenges?

It's all down to **mind over matter**.

A winning mindset comes from having the right attitude and will determine your future.

KEY MESSAGES

MIND OVER MATTER
Your attitude will determine your future

- Success often depends on having the right mindset
- We need to forget about who we were and focus on who we can be
- Those with self-discipline and willpower actively try to control their own future
- The opposite of winning is losing
- The opposite of success is failure
- To win in life you should never stop learning
- Excellence is more likely to be achieved if you strive for perfection
- 'Tough times don't last. Tough people do.'
- Failure isn't falling down – it's staying down
- The lows test us and are necessary to fully appreciate the highs
- Learn from your mistakes
- Good often comes from adversity
- A winning mindset comes from having the right attitude and will determine your future

CHAPTER 4

THE HUB

Managing yourself to maximise your effectiveness

The *Little Oxford Dictionary* defines the hub as '*a central part of a wheel, from which spokes radiate*'.

Being chief executive of your own life, having your own vision and goals is exciting. But, as in the **Nelson Mandela** quote earlier, we should constantly remind ourselves that:

'Vision without action is only a dream.'

The actions required to make your dream reality are the real challenge and are what I describe as **'the hub** of my working life'. These actions require strong self-discipline and learning to manage yourself effectively, as I learnt very early on in my management career.

Mark had asked me with very little notice to join the board of Hambro Life and become its sales director. I had joined the company at its launch five years earlier, having previously worked for three years at Mark's first company, Abbey Life.

At the age of 33 my management experience was very limited. It certainly hadn't involved running a sales force of 1,700 self-employed people considerably older than me. It was an exciting – but daunting – prospect.

What I remember from those first weeks was being inundated with requests from the salespeople and their managers for one-to-one meetings, as well as their numerous phone calls to the 'new kid on the block'.

The main purpose behind the meeting requests and phone calls was to lobby me on their own particular hobby horses (mainly to improve their financial benefits!) which had rightly been rejected by my predecessor.

For the first time in my life I found my new role was stressful. I felt pressure from the mound of paper that accumulated on my desk and from not being in control of how I used my time as I reacted to events.

The personal coach I mentioned earlier, Jinny Ditzler, came to my rescue. She convinced me that I had to take responsibility for my life and have very clear goals each month in order to achieve my vision. In other words, **I had to take control of my life rather than have it control me.**

What follows is what I call 'the hub of my working life'.

THE HUB OF MY WORKING LIFE

On the last Sunday of each month I review (usually with the aid of a glass of scotch in the evening) how I have done against the objectives I set myself for the month.

I analyse what has gone well and what I have achieved – but also, just as importantly, what has gone less well and why.

In other words, what lessons can I learn and what do I need to change or do differently going forward?

I then focus on what my key objectives should be for the following month which, if achieved, would make next month a great month for me. **The key is only to have objectives for actions that you don't have to do anyway**, otherwise you won't achieve anything because you are merely listing what's in your diary anyway.

Those key objectives ensure that I'm proactive rather than reactive during the month, focusing on my priorities rather than just reacting to events as they occur.

While the majority of the objectives I set myself are to ensure that I keep on track to hit my goals, it is just as important to maintain the goals I've already achieved. These objectives, typically 7–10 in number, I list on a sheet of paper under the heading:

A great month for Mike Wilson

It will list my business objectives for the month, which might include:

❏ preparing a talk which I'm due to give in six weeks' time

❏ preparing for the one-to-one meetings scheduled for the month.

Having learnt from my mistakes in the past in my personal life, it will always have:

❏ Seeing Panda, my daughter, and grandchildren during the month,

and may also include for example:

❏ Booking (and keeping!) four sessions with my personal trainer

❑ Inviting friends out to dinner

❑ Booking a holiday for Christmas.

Importantly, I check with Sophie what should be included to make the month great from her point of view.

I always aim to include one non-time-critical objective, such as tidying my office at home, knowing that if I don't, I will never get around to it.

During the month I tick off my objectives as they are achieved, not leaving everything to be done on the last day of the month!

I know that if I can hit, say, 8 out of 10 of my monthly objectives then I have virtually **guaranteed** myself a great month. Before I started setting my objectives for each month, I would often reflect on the previous month and be disappointed with the outcome. This was hardly surprising because I hadn't worked out in **advance** what would actually have made it a good month. I now find that, when I look back over the previous month, I am happy with how it went almost every time.

This regular exercise enables me to focus on the purpose of each month, to be better organised and use my time as effectively as possible. I now have a good work/life balance and am, hopefully, easier to live with.

DAILY ROUTINE

Building a daily routine into your business life is beneficial and a good discipline – even if it is only for the start and end of each day. A daily routine becomes a habit, and self-discipline comes through habit.

If you follow sport and go, for example, to Twickenham for a rugby international, or to watch a Premiership football match, you will always see the players doing their warm-up routine before the game itself. The reason for this is obvious.

I believe that I benefit from having **my own warm-up routine** at the start of each working day.

I have a daily routine of 15–20 minutes maximum that gives me the best chance of being able to achieve what I want to achieve by the end of the day. It makes me fit for purpose. It's not dissimilar to a pilot checking his dials before he takes off on his journey.

The first thing I do each day is to **check my list of objectives**, 'A great month for Mike Wilson', with a few of them hopefully already ticked off as achieved. I then remind myself of the outstanding objectives that will determine my actions for the rest of the month and ensure that I remain proactive.

I then **check my action list**, which I brought up-to-date at the end of the previous day, again as a matter of routine.

I have a very unsophisticated system for this list: one sheet with a line down the middle with 'phone calls to make' listed on the left-hand side, and 'things to do' on the right. I put an asterisk against the items I commit myself to completing that particular day.

The third thing I do is to **check for any items on my leather pocket pad** (which I have with me at all times). I may have agreed over dinner the night before to send someone something or to phone them the next day. If so, these actions are then added to my action list.

The last part of my daily routine at the start of each day is to **check my 'Brought-Forward' file**, where I keep emails or copies of memos or letters where I've requested a response or information. I ensure that outstanding responses are chased by my secretary and I feel that I benefit from the majority of recipients being aware that I operate this system and that there's no hiding place. I think they probably action my requests ahead of others, but that may be wishful thinking!

Anyway, I feel better doing this each day and feel more in control.

I always try to action the hardest tasks first, particularly making tricky telephone calls, on the basis that my day can only get better. My calls when I was in management weren't always welcomed!

I regret not being as disciplined as far as my health is concerned, in particular being a chain-smoker from the age of 18 until I reached 70, when I was diagnosed with lung cancer and moved onto electronic cigarettes. While you can't change your past you can have regrets about it! A major regret for me is my lack of attention to maintaining my good health as a priority.

I wish that I had appreciated a bit earlier that good physical health is more important than success in business and making money. I have generally been fairly disciplined as far as my diet is concerned, but what I have not done is to build a daily exercise routine into my life along similar lines to my working life routine.

My working routine has become a habit and is as natural to me as cleaning my teeth each morning. The reason I'm suggesting something along these lines is because several people have said to me: 'I'm not as self-disciplined as you so I'm not sure your ideas would work for me.'

I read somewhere that if you repeat something every day for a month it becomes a habit or routine – in other words the **self-discipline is limited to 30 days; after that it's second nature!**

'The chains of habit are too tight to be felt until they are too heavy to be broke.'

Samuel Johnson

CORRESPONDENCE

I haven't kept up with technology and I have my emails printed, and they and the post are sorted into categories: 'Urgent Action', 'Action' and 'Reading', and prioritised in that order.

Until I adopted this very obvious way of dealing with correspondence, I would write off far too much time ploughing through everything in no logical order. The task ahead always appeared more daunting than it actually was.

All 'Action' items are dealt with immediately or an acknowledgement is sent. My most valuable piece of office equipment is my Dictaphone (I'm not into technology!) and I dictate the majority of responses.

READING

All non-urgent reading – magazines, etc. – goes into my briefcase, which I keep with me at all times when I am out of the office. I read on the train, in a taxi or when I am early or kept waiting for an appointment. The latter is far less annoying if I can catch up on my reading – and almost becomes a positive.

I realise that I am behind on my reading when my briefcase becomes too heavy or is full. I should add that my briefcase is quite large and not a trendy slim one!

PHONE CALLS

My personal rule is to return all phone calls within 24 hours. However busy my day may be, there are always breaks in-between meetings when calls can be made. In reality, I find that the majority of my calls end up with me leaving a message that I returned the person's call because they themselves are in a meeting. That doesn't matter; at least I get the credit for having the courtesy to respond within 24 hours.

I find that I can only ensure that I do this by firstly transferring all phone messages onto my action list rather than accumulating slips of paper with phone messages, and secondly, by keeping my action list with me at all times.

MAIN CONTACTS SHEET

This is a very simple but effective system.

I have another single sheet of paper, this one with a line down the middle and three horizontal lines, creating nine boxes. In each box I put the name of one of the people I have most regular contact with. When I was Chief Executive this was Mark as Chairman, and my direct reports. I have a separate sheet for my secretary, Elizabeth.

As points occur during the day, I jot them down in the appropriate person's box for discussion with them or to ask them to action.

The benefits of operating this system are:

❏ When I make a telephone call to my main contacts, I have usually accumulated two or three points. This avoids me phoning someone about something as it occurs and minutes later phoning them back with a, 'Sorry, I forgot to mention', which is annoying to the recipient.

❏ When I receive a call from one of the main contacts on my sheet, I can give my full attention to what they are saying. Before I adopted this system, I was often only partially listening, while racking my brain for the points I wanted to talk to them about! They are now on the sheet in front of me and I merely say when they have finished their points, 'While you're on the phone, I have three quick points I'd like to discuss with you.'

This system really works well for me and maximises the efficiency of each call.

I operate a similar system for people I have regular one-to-one meetings with. As points occur between meetings, I list them on their individual file or plastic folder. This avoids me having to rely on my memory for everything, which inevitably means missing points.

There is a hidden agenda from my point of view in operating my main contacts sheet. I am a lousy delegator by nature and I realised some time ago that this shortcoming would significantly slow down the growth of the Company unless I found a way to overcome it.

The only way I've learnt to delegate and feel comfortable about doing so is to build in my own checking system for the important things that I delegate.

The major benefit to me of operating my main contacts sheet is that any actions I've delegated to individuals are only removed from their box when I have confirmation that they've been actioned.

I'm only too aware that if I agree to do or follow up on something for someone, it is actually irrelevant to that person whether I have delegated it to someone else or not. He or she holds me 100% accountable for delivery – and rightly so.

MY KEY FACILITATOR

My key facilitator is an outstanding secretary or PA whom I view as a major player in my team.

It is, however, all too easy not to maximise the potential of this relationship because of poor communication.

Think about how you interact with your secretary. If you only issue a series of instructions to your secretary or PA then things will be carried out, but you will miss out on the added value that they can provide for you.

The best way to test whether this is true is to reverse roles. Imagine you are your secretary. Do you think that you would be motivated and able to contribute more if your boss let you know:

❑ the current issues for the business; what was going well and less well?

❑ something about the people who are really important to him or her?

❑ your boss's hang-ups and foibles – as well, of course, as your boss being aware of yours?

Would you be able to perform better as a secretary if:

❑ your boss always discussed with you the work priorities for the day and week?

❏ your boss made an effort to understand and endeavoured to take this into account when allocating work to you – including avoiding giving you a tape to type at the end of the day and nothing in the morning when you had time on your hands?

Everyone performs better when they feel involved and valued and the occasional thank you and show of appreciation doesn't go amiss!

A boss/secretary relationship should be viewed as a partnership. My secretary, Elizabeth, is an extension of me and she handles many of the queries that are directed my way. Our routine towards the end of each day is to run through what's been actioned and what's outstanding. Elizabeth has her own list and lets me know what I can remove from mine.

CONTROL OF MY DIARY

I want to maximise the use of my time and to stay in control of my own diary and appointments. Elizabeth will take calls requesting a meeting and will respond that she wants to double-check with me before confirming the time.

The advantages of this are:

❏ It allows me to decide whether I actually want the meeting in the first place (often a phone call will suffice).

❏ It gives me the option with some people who like meetings for meetings' sake to only offer a meeting in unsociable hours – very early or late in the day. I find many say that they will come back to confirm when and we don't hear from them again – but at least I offered!

❏ I can ensure that in the majority of cases the maximum time booked for a meeting is one hour and that the person is told this in advance. This ensures time is not taken up with small talk. Elizabeth puts her head round the door after an hour as a reminder that time's up.

❏ By controlling my own diary and appointments, I am able to avoid back-to-back meetings all day with no meaningful gaps. I feel that if I didn't do this the quality of the meetings would deteriorate during the day, allowing no time before or after meetings to gather my thoughts.

I used to fill my diary with meetings. **I now include appointments with myself** to prepare for a meeting or to write a talk.

In my experience the best or most effective meetings or talks are, in the majority of cases, down to preparation rather than any other single factor.

Preparation pays, and I view booking diary time for me to prepare as equally important to other appointments in my diary.

The number of meetings is less important than the quality of meetings.

Controlling my diary also enables me to compartmentalise things, which in turn leads to a better work/life balance.

THE BENEFITS OF COMPARTMENTALISATION

How many times have you heard people say 'my personal life does not affect my business life'?

Sadly, this is very rarely true. Problems or issues in your personal life almost inevitably have a negative effect on your business life. None of us are immune from this but the key is to try to minimise the effect.

Compartmentalising has a major role to play in minimising the impact of your personal life on your business life.

I have found that allocating a time slot in my diary to address a particular personal issue is enormously beneficial – in the same way it is for a business issue. The best example I can give is when I was about to become divorced.

There is never a good time for something like this to occur, but J. Rothschild Assurance had only been up and running for three years. I needed to focus on the business with no distractions.

At my first meeting with my divorce lawyer, Raymond Tooth, I asked him to act for me but only if we could have a clear understanding of how we would work together. I made it clear that I wanted to be in control of my diary:

❑ I wouldn't look at any of his correspondence to me until after 6.30pm.

❑ We would not phone each other during the working day – again, only after 6.30pm.

❑ All our meetings would take place in the evening.

Raymond Tooth readily agreed – his words were, 'Your requests are music to my ears'! He explained that the majority of his clients were women who wanted prime time during the day and my request suited him perfectly.

He did say, however, that he'd never had a request such as mine before and asked me to explain my reasoning. I said it was very straightforward: I wanted to address my divorce issues after work, and I wanted the very minimum of distraction during my working day so that I could focus on my business.

I explained that this would not be the case if I were dealing with meetings, letters or phone calls from him during the day. I knew that I'd probably view any requests from my (now-ex-) wife's lawyers as unreasonable (whether they were or not), which would put me in the wrong frame of mind for the rest of the day. He understood.

This is only one example and hopefully you won't face similar circumstances. I try to compartmentalise most aspects of both my business and personal life. I feel this enables me to focus 100% on what I am doing at the time, rather than juggling too many balls in the air.

Controlling my diary enables me to compartmentalise things.

A GOOD MEMORY CAN BE A PITFALL

When I was younger I took pride in having a good memory. The danger of this was that I didn't feel that it was necessary for me to write points down; it had become a personal challenge to remember everything.

Three things made me drop that challenge:

The first occurred in my business life. The time of a seminar I was speaking at was changed to an earlier time. I thought I'd remember. I forgot and never got there to give my talk. I felt I had let everyone down – and I had.

On the second occasion, at the end of a rather boring meeting – albeit on an important topic – I was unexpectedly asked for my opinion on a point and I could not respond. I realised that I had not been paying full attention because my mind was preoccupied with trying to remember what I had to do in the short time between the end of that meeting and my next one.

I had not been 100% focused on the meeting discussion; I let myself down and everyone knew it.

The third is an example in my personal life. I had agreed to give Mary, my then wife, a lift home to Gloucestershire from the hairdresser in London. We were giving a dinner party at home that evening. I relied on my memory and didn't write it down. Mark and I had been in a meeting and he asked for a lift to Gloucestershire so that we could continue our discussions.

It was a Friday afternoon so we left the office early to avoid rush hour. We were halfway down the M4 when Mary phoned to say that she was waiting for me outside the hairdresser in London!

Following her train journey home the hostess arrived after the guests – although her hair did look good! However, the dinner party was not a great success.

None of these things would have happened if I had not just relied on my memory.

I find the joy of writing down everything that I intend to do is that I can then forget about it, which enables me to sleep well at night. It's a commitment that it will actually happen. I referred earlier to my leather pocket pad that I have with me at all times for the same reason.

One final point on the potential pitfalls of relying on your memory:

I am astounded by how often, when I glance over and see people's papers for a meeting, there are no underlining or markings. They either have brilliant memories or, more likely, have merely skimmed the papers hoping to recall the key points.

I feel that, in either case, they are limiting the contribution they'll be able to make to any discussions. Back again to my belief that **preparation pays**.

THE MEANS TO AN END

Good personal organisation and self-discipline should be viewed as the hub of everything you do. The ability to manage yourself effectively is as important as managing others – and it's easier!

How can you effectively manage others if you can't manage yourself?

The most important attributes of leaders and successful business people are being authentic and trustworthy, focused and resilient, having good judgement, communication skills and building strong relationships in order to lead people.

These qualities are the spokes of the wheel which hopefully radiate from your hub! Without it, the wheel will not function.

This may sound a bit dramatic, but I am convinced of the value of being well-organised and using your time effectively.

If you are, then you are giving yourself the best chance of being able to focus on and excel at the more exciting key attributes to being successful.

A good personal hub will enable you to achieve your goals and realise your vision – with the added bonus of making your life less stressful.

The hub is a means to an end.

President Harry S. Truman once said:

> *'In reading the lives of great men, I find that the first victory they won was over themselves – self-discipline with all of them came first.'*

KEY MESSAGES

THE HUB
Managing yourself to maximise your effectiveness

- **Work out in advance what would make the following month a great month for you**
  - ⇨ set objectives for the month
- **Have a daily working routine for the start of each day. Check:**
  - ⇨ your objectives for the month
  - ⇨ your action list – asterisk the items you are committed to completing that day
  - ⇨ your pocket pad for any actions
  - ⇨ your brought-forward file
- **Sort your correspondence into categories:**
  - ⇨ Urgent Action
  - ⇨ Action
  - ⇨ Reading
- **Reading:**
  - ⇨ take non-urgent reading with you – don't look at it in the office
- **Phone calls:**
  - ⇨ return within 24 hours
  - ⇨ transfer all calls onto an action list and keep this with you at all times
- **Main contacts sheet:**
  - ⇨ sheet divided into boxes with names of people you have most contact with

- **Your key facilitator:**
  - ⇨ a secretary/PA is a major player in your team
  - ⇨ communicate with them, involve and show you value them
- **Control your own diary**
- **Compartmentalise the different aspects of your life**
- **A good memory can be a pitfall**
  - ⇨ write things down
- **Have a daily physical exercise routine**
  - ⇨ maintaining good health should be a high priority
- **View good personal organisation and self-discipline as the hub of everything you do. It will help to determine your future.**

CHAPTER 5

MEETINGS FOR MEETINGS' SAKE

Ensure you get value for money

ASK YOURSELF: WHAT PERCENTAGE of meetings you have attended over, say, the last three months, that achieved their goal, were worthwhile and memorable? Were they a good investment of your time, the time of those attending and the company's money?

Too little thought is often given to whether a particular meeting is actually required in the first place. Often meetings are fixed merely for meetings' sake – and this applies to all types of meetings, large, small or one-to-ones.

The key questions to ask are:

❑ is a meeting actually required?

If so,

❑ for how long?

❑ what is the purpose of the meeting?

❑ who should attend?

If you are arranging any meeting, a good discipline is to commit yourself **in advance** as to what you would like to be able to say **after** the meeting in terms of what made it worthwhile, rather than rationalise after the event.

Ask yourself: 'What do **I** want out of the meeting?' What do you want the **attendees** to get out of the meeting? Could yours and their time have been used more productively to drive the business forward?

Meetings are an investment of people's time and that costs real money in terms of the salaries of those attending and, in many cases, travel costs. Do a back-of-the-envelope calculation of the total costs to remind yourself from time to time, because the costs won't be shown in the company's management accounts. Are you achieving real value for money?

LARGE MEETINGS

These may be for 20+ attendees, or perhaps everyone within your company (5,000+). While hopefully engaging your audience, you will nevertheless be largely talking **at** them as you impart information.

Many people are more comfortable and are better at presenting to large numbers rather than running small meetings or one-to-ones, which require a different skillset. While numerous training courses and books are available on giving speeches and presentations, far fewer are available on running effective small meetings and one-to-ones, even though they occur far more frequently in day-to-day business.

SMALL MEETINGS

These could be team or department meetings, or board meetings, when the opportunity exists with smaller numbers to get the attendees to participate actively, to gain their views and feedback. Not to do so and to talk at them would frustrate those attending and, importantly, would not enable you to gauge their reactions.

I remember attending my first BAT board meeting. The board papers had been sent out in advance. These included the Chairman's Report. To my astonishment, the chairman opened the board meeting by reading out his report (which we had all already read) verbatim to the board and, to make it worse, he didn't even read particularly well. It won't surprise you to hear that BAT board meetings were one-way traffic with little or no participation or feedback encouraged.

An effective chair will run worthwhile meetings. He or she will prepare well in advance by:

❏ setting the agenda (avoiding too many items)

❏ allocating the agenda items to specific individuals

❏ often asking for certain papers in advance of the meeting to save time in the meeting itself, but also to allow people to ask for more information or clarification prior to the meeting.

At the meeting itself an effective chair will, where necessary, explain at the outset the purpose of the meeting. He or she will set the scene:

❏ For certain agenda items they should make it clear that they are **not seeking a decision at the meeting** itself. This has the advantage of taking the pressure off the chair to meet any expectations of a decision on the spot which they may subsequently regret.

❑ They should **avoid the temptation to express their own views first** in discussions in order to encourage individuals to put forward theirs.

❑ They should **welcome and encourage challenge**. Unless they do so, the attendees will not feel that their own views will be considered when arriving at decisions. They may joke among themselves that the minutes may as well be handed out in advance of the meeting.

A skilful chair will orchestrate the entire meeting. They will:

❑ take all papers as read

❑ manage the time allocated to each item

but also, very importantly,

❑ manage the attendees

❑ ensure that the meeting starts and finishes on time, which often means continually forcing the momentum and moving things along.

The chair will draw out individual views rather than allow the herd instinct to prevail, while at the same time ensuring that no individual dominates the meeting with their personal views or particular hobby horse.

It's a fact of life that many people are lazy by nature and, sadly, they will often have given little or no thought in advance of the meeting to points to be discussed.

If, however, they know that a particular chair's style is to seek individual views on topics, they will prepare in advance rather than be caught out.

BLACK HAT, WHITE HAT

For certain agenda items on topics such as product developments, try using what I will call the **Black Hat, White Hat** exercise, which is a worthwhile discipline.

Let's look at how this works when, for example, a new product is presented in a paper in advance of the meeting itself. People then have to put on their **Black Hat** – when they are only allowed to express their **negative** points or reservations about the products for, say, half an hour. These points are shown on a flip chart. No one is allowed to counter these views with positives or to disagree.

This is followed by people putting on their **White Hat,** for the same amount of time, when **only positives** can be expressed for the product and again put up on a flip chart. No one is allowed to counter with negatives, reservations or disagree. They have already had their opportunity to do this when wearing their **Black Hat**.

Clearly it is important to get the order of wearing the hats the right way around, ending with the positives.

This exercise, in my experience, largely avoids the inevitable friction during a discussion on, say, product development, between the marketeers and salespeople, and the financial guardians who, quite understandably, will home in on costs rather than sales. They both still have the opportunity to make their points as strongly as they like but in a structured way that is likely to produce a far better outcome.

I've learnt from experience that there are considerable advantages to facing up to negative points of view first – and this often works in life as in business.

I have never particularly relished – or been good at – giving talks, preferring an exchange of views and ideas with attendees. I used to limit my talk to a maximum of 20 minutes at Partner office meetings around the country, followed by an open forum or question-and-answer session, which I really enjoyed. My only frustration was when the initial, often very positive, atmosphere and discussion was dampened by a Partner raising an administrative error – such as for his or her client, Major Snooks, whose change of address had not been picked up. While an individual's case such as this was rarely of particular interest to other attendees, it would inevitably prompt a few others to cite similar examples they had experienced with their clients. Very quickly, the atmosphere in the meeting would change for the worse and it would become a challenge to re-establish a positive environment.

At one particular office meeting I had been warned in advance that the mood in the camp was not good. The economy was poor and securing new business for Partners was tough; regulation and compliance were becoming an increasing burden on them, while at the same time our administration centre was not performing well. Clearly, this was not a great scenario for self-employed financial advisers such as our Partners.

I decided to tackle this by acknowledging in my 20-minute talk that we all faced a number of challenges which we would overcome together. In the open forum that followed, for the first time I asked the Partners to wear their black hats and tell me all the negatives that they were experiencing and what SJP could do to help. No positive comments were allowed – and there weren't any!

Then they were asked to wear their white hats and only to bring up positives about SJP. I couldn't believe how well this worked: the Partners themselves put things into perspective and came up with numerous examples of how the Company was great and still in a different league to their previous companies or competitors. The meeting atmosphere was transformed.

I was amazed and continued this exercise on many other occasions.

Just a word of warning: it would have been a great mistake not to follow up after the meeting on the negatives raised just because the meeting ended on such a positive note.

WAR GAMES

At least once a year, perhaps at the annual strategy day meeting, it's worth considering allocating sufficient time to play **War Games**.

In these, the attendees are asked to assume that they are on the board of their current main competitor or new potential competitor. The exercise is for the attendees to put themselves in the competitor's shoes and to work out what tactics or strategy they would adopt to protect their position, in the case of the main competitor, or to compete with your own company, in the case of the new potential competitor.

The benefit of carrying out the exercise is to be fully prepared and to avoid complacency.

1. All attendees have to ensure that they are fully aware of the current strengths and weaknesses of your main competitor or potential competitor (perhaps a new entrant into your market).

2. Only then can they try to anticipate what your competitors are likely to do to compete against you and act accordingly.

The **Black Hat, White Hat** exercise and **War Games** are good examples of the benefits that smaller, more interactive meetings have over larger ones where the attendees are solely being presented to, as they enable attendees to participate and express their views.

ONE-TO-ONE MEETINGS

One-to-one meetings go one step further, as these meetings rely on active participation by both parties for them to be of any value.

There are various types of one-to-ones with different purposes and objectives. The most common are:

❏ transactional one-to-ones

❏ developmental one-to-ones

❏ one-to-ones where both transactions and personal development are covered.

While most people will allocate sufficient time to prepare for large and small meetings, this is often not the case for one-to-one meetings – which is a mistake as the quality and value of these meetings will suffer as a result.

As with other meetings, one-to-one meetings should be scheduled with a start and end time. This is to ensure both parties prepare in advance and that there's a clear focus on what's important to discuss in the time available.

I suggest as a guideline to allow:

❑ half an hour for a transactional-only meeting

❑ one hour for a developmental-only meeting

❑ one-and-a-half hours for meetings covering transactional and personal development (with transactions covered in the first half hour).

People often tell me that they find half an hour insufficient time in monthly one-to-ones to cover transactions. This is usually the case because there is little or no communication about the various transactions in-between one-to-one meetings. If both parties agree to give email updates between one-to-ones rather than waiting to do so face-to-face at their next meeting, time in the meeting can be freed up to focus on the most important transactions from that month.

Meetings should start on time and you should not cancel or postpone one-to-ones unless it is unavoidable. While, unlike other meetings, it only affects one person if you do, you are running the risk of them not feeling valued by you.

A major focus for any boss, mentor or coach should be to develop and inspire people to perform better (or even better) in the future. You do not get the best out of people by criticising their shortcomings. You do so by convincing them that they are capable of being even better and improving their performance.

One-to-ones give you the best opportunity to do this on a regular basis and, if you are successful, the return on the investment of both your time will be inestimable.

Initial One-to-One

The **agenda for the initial one-to-one** you have with someone should be:

❑ establishing the ground rules and expectations of both of you for your subsequent meetings

❑ you getting to know the person better as an individual, which will give you a greater chance to help him or her to perform better and to realise their full potential.

It is important to know the following:

❑ What is their family situation, their wife's, husband's or partner's name as well as the ages and names of any children they may have?

❑ What are their hobbies or interests?

❑ What have been their successes, failures or disappointments in the past?

❑ What do they view as their particular strengths or weaknesses?

❑ What are their values?

❑ What motivates them most; what is their 'hot button'?

And, very importantly:

❏ What is important to them and what are their ambitions and goals for the future?

❏ What is their three-year vision?

A permanent record should be kept of the individual's personal information for all your future meetings. While the format for the various one-to-ones you have with different people may be very similar, they should be personalised and tailored to each individual.

Most people are not able to articulate their three-year vision (including all aspects of their life, both business and personal) in the initial one-to-one meeting. When this is the case I ask them to work on developing their three-year vision so that we can discuss it at our next meeting.

I suggest that a starting point could be carrying out an audit on all key aspects of their current life today and visualising what they would like the audit to look like in three years' time. This should be stretching but at the same time realistic.

Future One-to-Ones

The second one-to-one should focus on the person's three-year vision with you asking questions to ensure, as far as possible, that they have considered all aspects of their life and are really committed to achieving their vision. Ask them to visualise how they will feel if their vision becomes reality. If they don't appear excited then they won't be motivated to achieve it and they almost certainly need to reassess what their three-year vision should be.

The benefit of persuading someone to focus on a vision for themselves in three years' time (rather than – or as well as – their longer-term vision) is that because of the short timescale immediate action is required in order to achieve it.

Once their vision is finalised, then move on to agreeing what their goals should be for the next 12 months – their stepping stones – so as to be on track to achieve it. In subsequent one-to-ones, I then encourage them to visualise at the end of each month a great month for themselves for the following month by listing, say, 7–10 objectives (both business and personal) in their own time which, if achieved, would make it a great month for them. (See Chapter 4 for more explanation of how I plan for a great month.)

All future one-to-ones start with how they've done against their objectives or goals for the month:

❏ why any were missed

❏ what went well during the month

❏ what went poorly

❏ what, if any, lessons were learnt.

And, as a result of the above, what will they change or do differently in the future?

Depending on their answers to these questions I will then try to persuade them to focus on, for example:

❏ their personal organisation and self-discipline

❏ establishing a daily routine

❑ controlling their own diary

❑ compartmentalising different aspects of their life.

If they are in a leadership role then it may include focusing on:

❑ their attributes as a leader

❑ how they are treating their people (reminding them that people perform best when they feel that they are valued, respected, cared for and appreciated)

❑ their personal brand

❑ culture.

Remember: you cannot inspire others unless you are inspired yourself.

The challenge is to ensure that all meetings – large, small or one-to-ones – are worthwhile and memorable as well as inspirational. If they are, then they will be an excellent investment of your time and the company's money and they will not be perceived as meetings for meetings' sake.

KEY MESSAGES

MEETINGS FOR MEETINGS' SAKE
Ensure you get value for money

- **How many meetings are a good investment?**
  - ⇨ Assess the cost in terms of your time and those attending
  - ⇨ Is a meeting actually required?
- **Different skillsets are required depending on the size and purpose of the meeting**
- **An effective chair will prepare well in advance and explain at outset the purpose of the meeting**
  - ⇨ the chair will orchestrate the entire meeting
- **The Black Hat, White Hat exercise:**
  - ⇨ negatives followed by positives
- **Play War Games:**
  - ⇨ what tactics or strategy would you adopt to compete with your own company?
  - ⇨ anticipate in order to act accordingly
- **One-to-one meetings:**
  - ⇨ prepare as much as for large meetings
  - ⇨ know as much as possible about the person
  - ⇨ split between transactional and personal development
- **Avoid meetings for meetings' sake**

CHAPTER 6

YOUR TITLE DOESN'T MAKE YOU A LEADER

Followship and inspiring people does

WHEN I WAS 30, my burning ambition was to join the board of Hambro Life by the time the company was targeted to go public three years later. I wanted to be in the prospectus!

I achieved my ambition when I was appointed sales director in 1976 (the year we went public). I naively assumed that my title alone would automatically make me a leader. It didn't take me long to appreciate that nothing could be further from the truth, and that people weren't going to follow me just because of my position or job description.

I soon realised that I had to earn the right to be the leader of the sales force. I had to prove myself, gain their respect and, most importantly, I had to win their hearts and minds.

I knew that my success as a leader would depend on getting results through others, and that a leader is only as good as his people. In order to win their hearts and minds, to inspire them to follow me, and at times to convince people what they viewed as impossible was possible, I knew that I needed the following **key attributes**:

❏ **Authenticity and trustworthiness** – I didn't want people to be asking themselves: 'Is it more about him than us?'

❏ **The ability to build strong relationships** – I had to build a strong relationship with both my management team and as many of our salespeople as possible as quickly as possible.

❏ **The ability to exercise sound judgement and decision-making**.

❏ **The ability to communicate well**.

It became clear that a leader's role is to **lead** and **inspire** people to achieve the company's goals and vision. To do this, I had to have the right attitude; I needed to have a winning mindset. It was important to focus on what would really make a difference – which meant I had to have self-discipline, be well-organised and resilient.

I quickly learnt the key differences between a manager and a leader.

A MANAGER	A LEADER
Manages	Leads
Maintains	Develops
Accepts status quo	Challenges
Is largely reactive	Is proactive
Relies on control	Inspires trust
Is a classic 'good soldier'	Is their own boss

There are many capable managers who can manage aspects of the business better than a leader can, and any business needs both. I learnt to appreciate that a leader's job is very different.

The starting point was to create my own vision for the sales force going forward; a vision which Mark and the key players would buy into. Mark was my sounding board every Tuesday morning at our one-to-ones.

Hambro Life already had the most successful sales force in the UK but still wasn't performing to its full potential.

It lacked team spirit and a sense of belonging. Also, many of our self-employed salespeople purported to be IFAs (Independent Financial Advisers) and often recommended the products of our competitors. Some had their own businesses outside financial services and were in reality part-time with Hambro Life.

The consequence of this was that:

1. our recruitment standards were poor,

   as was

2. productivity per salesperson

   and

3. the sales force turnover rate was high.

We were playing the numbers game (like others), which was both costly and damaging to our image and reputation. Many changes were needed if I was to achieve my vision of **building a high-quality and productive sales force**.

As a **manager** I was not in a position to change the fundamentals; as a **leader** I was accountable and could.

This brought home to me more than anything else the big difference between managing and leading.

Over time, a number of senior sales managers had to be replaced. The key performance indicators (KPIs) were changed for both the remuneration of sales management and the incentives and recognition for our salespeople.

These major changes were initially viewed with suspicion. How best to communicate them was as challenging as actually making the changes.

In my first full year as sales director, the size of the sales force fell significantly for the first time, but fortunately our new business and profits increased.

KEY ATTRIBUTES OF AN EFFECTIVE LEADER

BEING AUTHENTIC AND TRUSTWORTHY

If your people don't perceive you as being genuine and trust-worthy, it will limit your ability to build strong relationships, and will also severely dilute any other key attributes you may have.

As much as people want you to lead by example and to set standards, they need you to be truly yourself, and to show some humility. They don't want you to succumb to delusions of grandeur, to get carried away with your status, to posture, be full of self-importance or to see you strutting around the place. They don't expect their leader to be superhuman – so don't pretend you are or that you have all the answers; they know that you will have strengths and weaknesses (although hopefully not fatal flaws!). Great leaders aren't afraid to be fallible and they keep their egos under control. They don't have a burning desire to be in the spotlight all the time.

Mark was high-profile and a legend before the launch of

J. Rothschild Assurance, having founded two life assurance companies – Abbey Life and Hambro Life. Although we were joint founders of JRA, it would have been foolhardy not to have capitalised on his reputation and standing in our industry.

It never entered my head to try to be in the external spotlight myself. All I wanted was the respect of our internal people, and of the Partnership in particular.

It was Mark whom we promoted externally as the face of JRA. Our PR interviews with journalists and potential shareholders were his domain. He opened our offices around the country, launched new products and chaired our internal investment conferences. He was far better qualified than me to fulfil these roles, while I focused on building our team and culture, Partnership recruitment and motivating people. Our respective roles of Chairman and Chief Executive were irrelevant – we capitalised on our individual strengths and it never concerned us who was in the spotlight at any particular time externally or internally.

Good leaders channel their personal ambitions into their company and people. Their satisfaction comes from the achievements of their team rather than what they personally have achieved.

While people want to be able to relate to their leader, this does not mean they have to like them. A leader's priority should be to be respected rather than to be liked. To achieve both should be viewed as a bonus!

Leaders are seen to be genuine and respected for their actions rather than their words. Just talking a good game is not sufficient.

❑ Saying, for instance, 'our assets are our people' and not treating them as such will be seen as no more than the use of clever rhetoric.

❏ Constantly using the words 'to be honest' gives the impression that, for the rest of the time, you're not.

❏ Consistency between your words and your deeds will instil trust in your people.

Always be sure to do the following:

❏ do what you say you will do

❏ under-promise and over-deliver (say 'I'll come back to you in 48 hours' and do so in 24)

❏ lead by example; you are a role model

❏ practise what you preach.

If you execute as promised you will be seen as the leader your people trust, respect and want to follow.

MAKING TOUGH DECISIONS

Doing what is best for the company often involves making tough decisions. The toughest ones involve individuals – and their futures.

The best interests of the company had to be the overriding priority in order to achieve the vision of Hambro Life building a high-quality and productive sales force. This could only be delivered by having the highest-quality sales management team, which inevitably meant casualties along the way.

The decision as to who had to be replaced was relatively easy – who replaced them was harder – but the toughest bit was delivering the news to the individuals. I was very close to several of the people at Hambro Life, having known them for years. I knew their families, often having been on holidays with them and, in one case, having been best man at their wedding. But I realised that I had to compartmentalise friendship and business. If I allowed my friendship to influence my decision then I would lose the trust and respect of our team.

Very importantly, making tough decisions does not mean being tough in the delivery of the news to the person – in fact, just the opposite. People often said to me that they didn't envy me having to break the news to the individual. However, I always reminded myself that it might be tough on me, but that was nothing compared to what it was like for those on the receiving end.

Thorough preparation for the meeting was essential in order to anticipate his or her likely reaction. Apart from the obvious issue of the financial terms, how was their leaving going to be announced internally and externally? I was also very aware that they faced the difficult task of telling their wife or husband the largely unexpected news.

On one occasion, towards year end, the decision had been made that someone would have to leave. I decided I would do this at our next one-to-one before I went away over Christmas, rather than have it hanging over me and in the back of my mind. Fortunately, I appreciated only just in time that I was being selfish, because a difficult hour-long meeting for me was nothing compared to what he would be facing after I broke the news to him, with Christmas coming up and he and his family looking forward to their own holiday abroad. I rearranged the meeting for January when we were both back.

With very few exceptions I am still in touch with most of the people I asked to leave – in particular those who were the result of my own recruitment errors or who had given of their best but had been promoted above their own level of competence. Neither was their fault.

It was the delivery of the bad news, rather than making those tough decisions, that affected people; that was really the worst part of my job as leader. The important thing to me was to do as much as possible to maintain the individuals' dignity and self-esteem.

BUILDING STRONG RELATIONSHIPS

It is essential that you are authentic in order to build a strong and trusted relationship between you and your team. That relationship will largely determine the future success – or otherwise – of your company. If you want respect from your team it is important to show that you respect them. **Show respect to gain respect.**

To cement these relationships, you need to cultivate a number of skills, which I will now discuss in more detail.

Know Your People and What Motivates Each One of Them

The starting point must be to know and understand the key members of your team: what drives them, what are their values and dreams as well as their individual strengths and weaknesses. Only when you understand them will you see their potential, help to bring it out, and will both of you be able to benefit from what they are capable of contributing.

Years ago, I was running a sales management workshop at Hambro Life about the importance of relationships. One of the sessions was: 'How well do you know your team?'

The sales managers were asked to list the following about their top six salespeople:

❑ family situation (wife, husband or partner's name and number of children)

❑ hobbies and interests

❑ ambitions for the future

❑ skills, motives and key values

❑ what made each of their top salespeople tick – what was their 'hot button'?

Much to my surprise, after half an hour or so, the majority of managers were looking uncomfortable and clearly struggling with this very simple exercise.

It was clear that this group of sales managers knew very little about the key members of their teams. Yet these people were their most valuable assets, whose performance largely determined whether they hit their targets for the year and hence determined their own remuneration.

The top salespeople at Hambro Life had constantly questioned the value of their managers and resented the amount they earned on the back of them. This workshop brought home to me why.

It was clear that the salespeople were being taken for granted and that there was little or no relationship between them and their managers. They neither had the respect of their people nor had they won their hearts and minds. They weren't leaders by any stretch of the imagination and this was slowing down our sales growth as a company.

The 'How well do you know your team?' session reflected what I focused on, both with my own sales management team and with the top salespeople – particularly those qualifying for our overseas conventions.

Throughout my working life I have realised that preparation really does pay. As well as double-checking that I could put names to faces and remember the salesperson's own partner's name, I would do the obvious things such as:

❏ Greet them at the airport as they came off the plane – in those days often actually being allowed onto the tarmac to do so.

❏ Ensure that I invited top salespeople to my table when we had a formal seating plan. The seating plan itself was important, so I specified this and obviously made sure that my wife was fully briefed as to who was on our table and who was sitting next to her.

❏ We always gave each salesperson's partner a small gift on the final night of the convention. Rather than put these with the place card on their table, I would go around to every table handing these out personally, which gave me the opportunity to thank them for their support.

I was fortunate that other companies viewed their sales force very differently to us and had very different relationships. The directors would often distance themselves from their salespeople and would have their own separate top table for their company dinners.

I was always conscious that without these top salespeople we didn't have a business and that they should never be taken for granted.

The conventions were an ideal opportunity to make them feel special, valued, respected, cared for and appreciated.

How can you possibly build a strong relationship with your key people if you don't know anything about them? An effective leader will have found out what motivates each key individual in their team. They won't fall into the trap of assuming that they are all motivated by the same thing. The incentive of a Top Performers' Dinner held on a Friday night may well work for some, but we are all different and, for many, the prospect of a late night and starting the weekend with a hangover won't appeal to them – let alone to their families! For them, a dinner with their wife, husband or partner might appeal more and would still recognise their contribution as the top performer.

While an effective leader will know and build strong relationships with their direct reports and key people, it is clearly not possible with everyone, particularly in a large company.

Putting Names to Faces

It is beneficial to be able to put names to as many people as possible so as to make them feel recognised and important to you. Some people find putting names to faces easier to do than others and, as I said earlier, leaders are human like everyone else and have their own individual strengths and weaknesses.

In the same way that giving speeches to large audiences has never been one of my strong points, Mark would be the first to say that putting names to faces has never been his. Yet he, more than anyone, appreciated the value of all our people as assets even if he forgot their individual names at times. It was Mark who taught me how to arrive, for example, at a capital value for each of our salespeople based on a multiple of their potential future revenue/profit contribution for the Company each year.

At our Annual Company Meetings Mark would always be totally relaxed delivering a brilliant talk, but he was less relaxed at the drinks and dinner that followed. I was the other way around and it is one of the reasons our partnership together worked so well.

I remember on one occasion Mark coming up to me at the drinks before dinner and saying that he would need my help with the names. So I took Mark over to one of our longest-standing and very successful salesmen, Keith Bill, and said:

'Mark, you know Keith Bill.'

Mark greeted him. 'Of course I do – great to see you Bill.'

Keith Bill's response was: 'Mark, I hoped that after all these years we would be on Christian name terms.'

In fairness to Mark I have also had similar embarrassing moments over names.

One of the first conventions I hosted was in Acapulco. On the long flight I studied the booklet *Who's Who on the Convention*, which had photographs of all the qualifiers with the name of their guest. By the time we landed I was confident I could remember everyone's name and felt really good about it.

At the first night welcome drinks party, upon spotting our number one qualifier, I strolled over with confidence to say hello.

'John and Jane, great to see you both.'

My greeting was not met with the warmth I had anticipated – but with a thunderous look from John's guest. I quickly moved on only to learn later that John, at the last minute (after the booklet had been printed), had decided to invite Sally, his wife, to join him on the trip – rather than Jane, his long-standing girlfriend – in the hope of a reconciliation. My greeting clearly wasn't the best start to that process!

For the remainder of the drinks party I played safe and limited myself to greeting everyone the same way by just saying, 'Great to see you.'

For all future conventions I ensured that I was notified of any last-minute guest changes – you can always learn from your mistakes! Despite on occasion getting a person's name wrong, it is still worth the effort to put names to faces. People appreciate it and feel recognised and important to you.

Retaining the Right Distance

Effective leaders keep some sort of distance from their people, but are quick to offer the closest support if any of their people are in trouble. They engender strong relationships and loyalty from their people and balance being close and keeping enough distance to command respect.

There are circumstances when you need to empathise with your people and to sense their emotions – but not to the extent of becoming 'one of the boys' or 'girls', which will undermine their respect for you. You still have to keep your people focused, and address poor performance when it occurs.

At other times, leaders should be more distant from their people – but not to the extent that they separate themselves altogether and become isolated. If this occurs the danger is that they will only hear what people think they want to hear:

'Morale is high.'

'There are no issues.'

This false picture will inevitably have an adverse effect on their judgement and decision-making.

Exercising Sound Judgement and Decision-Making

The leader is ultimately accountable for all actions and decisions. But to be a strong leader doesn't necessitate being macho and making on-the-spot decisions.

Use colleagues as sounding boards before arriving at

significant decisions. You will not be seen as weak or as abnegating decisions when you do so, but respected for letting them challenge you and share the decision-making process with you in order to arrive at the right decision.

The worst decisions are usually poorly thought through and made in haste. How many decisions are truly time critical?

It is important to manage expectations. I will often start a meeting by saying that I want to hear everyone's views but, importantly, point out that we won't be arriving at a final decision today.

The Quality and Communication of Decisions Is What Counts

It is important to acknowledge that issues won't go away. You will be assessed by your people on the quality of your decisions and how they are communicated – not on your image or the speed of your decisions.

Preparation pays. Before arriving at any decisions of importance I will list the pros and cons of my provisional decision on the left- and right-hand sides of a sheet of paper. I do this to ensure I consider all the factors and can anticipate any consequences, as far as possible. Many decisions you make will inevitably be positive for one person (or group of people) but negative for others.

I always reverse roles and consider how I would react personally to my decision if I were in someone else's shoes. I then think through in advance what action I can take in order to capitalise on my decision with those who will benefit from it and minimise the adverse effect on those who will not. I ask myself whether, for example, I should communicate with them separately?

Going through this routine for any significant decisions determines how you can best communicate the decision and, at the same time, anticipate reactions to ensure that you have no surprises.

Many decisions are perceived as wrong and, while we have to accept that **perception is reality**, often what was wrong was not the decisions themselves but how they were communicated.

There is a tendency in all of us to arrive at a decision, feel a sense of relief and move on, when, in fact, only part of the job has been done.

As much – or more – time should be spent on deciding how to communicate a particular decision, as in making the decision itself.

Communicating Well

How you communicate with your people will shape their perception of you as their leader and your relationship with them.

> *'The single biggest problem with communication is the illusion it has taken place.'*

> George Bernard Shaw

All effective leaders will express clear goals and a vision for their company; they will demonstrate perseverance and display confidence. But the leader's goals and vision will only be achieved with the 100% support and commitment of their team and by recruits buying into and sharing the leader's vision.

Each team member will have their own role to play. How confident are you that they know exactly what you expect of them and the contribution they can make? Do they know your values, what's important to you and what you won't tolerate?

Your People's Role in Achieving Your Vision for Your Company

You should ask yourself how well you have communicated your company's goals and vision, and whether you have inspired your people sufficiently so that they are excited about playing their part in their company's future success and are focusing their energies in the same direction.

The price you pay for not doing so is enormous.

Here's a quote from an article on **building shareholder value**:

> *'Among those who don't understand their part in the big picture and believe they have little impact on results . . . only 23% are motivated to help the team achieve success.'*

In sharp contrast, the article goes on to say that the prize you gain from your people understanding their role and the personal impact they can make on results is that:

> *'91% are motivated to help the firm achieve success.'*

It is dangerous to assume that all your own team are motivated and committed because **you** think that you have communicated well with your people. The test is do **they** think you have communicated well?

Repetition will only reinforce how much you value your people and the important roles they need to play for the company to achieve success. This never does any harm.

Effective leaders will personally symbolise what their company stands for and communicate with conviction and passion. At the same time, they should not launch into monologues as if they know everything. They don't recruit or surround themselves with people who pretend to hang on their every word. They will encourage feedback about themselves and their company – both positive and negative. **A good leader is a great listener**.

> *'Make sure you hear what you don't want to hear.'*
>
> Feargal Quinn – founder of Superquinn

Effective leaders are well aware that communication is not just about delivering an inspiring speech or imparting information, but encouraging an open, two-way exchange of information.

Different Forms of Communication

Every day, leaders communicate in some form or other – whether this is to a large audience, in a small meeting, at a one-to-one, in a telephone conversation, or by written communication.

You should always assess what form of communication will be most effective for what you want communicated to your audience and whether you are the right person to communicate it. Different presentation skills are required for each form of communication.

The vital thing to avoid in any form of communication is using your position in the hierarchy to make a point. If you do, you are creating fear and will be perceived as being deeply insecure, intimidating or a bully.

Do not say: 'As chief executive I am telling you that this is how I want it done.'

Using this style of communication will destroy your relationship with your people and their perception of you as their leader.

Try Persuasion Before Telling

If you **tell** or issue orders as **the boss**, what do you do next if they are ignored? You have put yourself in a corner; you have nowhere to go. The use of persuasion, initially anyway, gives you far more scope for manoeuvre and you hopefully will never have to resort to telling.

COMMUNICATION STYLE

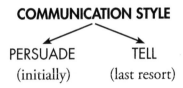

PERSUADE   TELL
(initially)   (last resort)

Communication through your body language also gives you the scope for manoeuvre.

People are more perceptive than we often give them credit for. Your facial expression will be noticed when you're in conversation or making a particular point.

If you naturally smile a lot most of the time, smiling less or not at all will indicate how important (or serious) you are about the point you're making. A look is often more powerful than words.

Smiling a lot can occasionally be misinterpreted. The directors of BAT challenged Mark's recommendation that I should join the BAT board. They queried how I could smile so much and at the same time be serious about business!

Avoid Only Hearing the Feedback You Want to Hear

Some people build reputations for themselves of 'broadcasting on radio transmit' when they communicate – again, this is something to avoid.

Here is an example of one executive 'broadcasting on radio transmit' and only registering the feedback he wants to hear, and another executive who elicits genuine feedback from his people:

There was a directors' meeting following our Annual Company Meeting and feedback on the meeting was an item on the agenda.

The first executive said that the only feedback he had was that it was excellent. He had no other comments.

The second executive said that, on the whole, the feedback on the conference was very good, but that there were a few suggestions for improving the next one and ran through them.

The first executive's feedback was based entirely on his **own** views. He had been on 'radio transmit' and had **told** his people that the conference was a tremendous success. Communicating this way certainly inhibited or, even worse, excluded honest feedback from the attendees who feared being perceived as negative by their leader. In addition, he ran the risk of being perceived as self-congratulatory with his glowing comments on the Annual Meeting, which the directors them-selves had been responsible for organising, and its content.

The second executive's communication style had been to **ask** his people for **their** views on the conference – both good and bad. He deliberately avoided expressing his own views first. He wanted to elicit honest feedback and asked for any suggestions (while they were fresh in their minds) to improve the next meeting.

Unlike the first executive, his people were made to feel that their views really did count and that they were valued.

Ask Questions Rather Than Make Statements

The late, great Joel Joffe, who was a director of Hambro Life, taught me that asking questions, and often just listening to people, are effective forms of communication.

He pointed out that I showed my frustration and often ran out of steam when I made what he tactfully described as rambling statements, such as:

'You annoy your colleagues by turning up late for meetings. You give the impression at times that you haven't read all the papers, which results in you not making a meaningful contribution to discussions.'

I have now learnt to make the same points by way of **asking questions** which invite a response:

- ○ 'Why do you turn up late for meetings?'
- ○ 'How do you think your colleagues feel about this?'
- ○ 'Do you feel you allow sufficient time to read all the papers and prepare for meetings – because you give the impression you don't?'
- ○ 'Do you feel you are making a meaningful contribution to discussions?'

Four responses required from four questions as opposed to no response from the original rambling statement!

Listen

There are times when you are not communicating points yourself, but are on the receiving end and listening to someone else's point of view. This, nevertheless, can also be an effective form of communication for you.

There are circumstances when people just want to vent their feelings to someone who will listen.

I have found this with financial advisers who occasionally

want to 'dump their bucket'. This could be about the administration's handling of an investment made by a client of theirs.

The one-way rant would end when they ran out of steam, with the adviser often saying, 'I apologise for that, but I feel so much better for having got that off my chest – thank you for listening.'

This brought home to me the point made earlier that I'd rather listen than be interrogated on various points!

Handwritten Letters and Cards

In today's world of the Internet, a handwritten letter or card is a rarity and because of this it is appreciated more by the recipient than ever before. Sending an email is an instant and efficient form of communication for the majority of correspondence. But speed should not be the sole criterion applied for all written communication. Examples of perfect opportunities for a handwritten response being:

❏ a thank you for dinner

❏ congratulations on a promotion

❏ wishing someone a speedy recovery from an illness

❏ sending condolences.

It will clearly have taken more thought and time to send a handwritten letter or card than to send an email. It is exactly for this reason that recipients will appreciate and value your more personal written communication, providing it is timely.

Emails

The senders of emails in business often forget that their emails should be consistent with the manner in which they communicate to the same person face-to-face. Just because the person is not visible should not change that. If it does, it will raise doubts in the person's mind about how genuine you are.

I did confess earlier to being a dinosaur as far as technology is concerned. What I didn't say is that this extends to me not actually doing my own emails but dictating them to Elizabeth. When doing so **I always try to visualise** the recipients of my emails and to see what I have said through their eyes.

I top and tail all my emails and try to start and end with pleasantries, with the 'meat' – or decision in this particular example – in the middle.

Example:

FROM: Mike Wilson

TO: Tom Burns

SUBJECT: CONCESSION

Tom,

I trust you are well.

I have read all the papers you sent me asking for a concession. I know you will be disappointed but considering all the circumstances – I do not feel that it's appropriate.

If, however, you feel that there's any additional information that would affect my decision then do please let me know.

I look forward to seeing you again soon.

Best wishes.

Mike Wilson

I could have written a far shorter email relaying the same decision:

FROM: Mike Wilson

TO: Tom Burns

SUBJECT: CONCESSION

I have read all the papers and I am not prepared to grant a concession.

Mike Wilson

The shorter email would obviously have taken less time and I would have cleared my desk more quickly – but it would not have been consistent with how I would have put over the decision in person. Despite the decision not being what Tom wanted to hear, I want to try to preserve my relationship with him, hence the longer email. Speed alone is not the essence.

Because maintaining good relationships is so important, before sending any email in the first place, I assess whether it is the most appropriate form of communication to use. I have witnessed too many email ping-pong matches severely damage relationships. Neither player would have communicated in the same blunt and impersonal manner expressed in their emails if, instead, they had met face-to-face or spoken over the phone to discuss their particular issue.

Many emails you send will not be addressed to one person, but to a particular group of individuals or to everyone in the company. Again, as with potentially sensitive individual emails, I always read a draft before sending. I used to reverse the roles; for example in the early days of J. Rothschild Assurance/St. James's Place I insisted on seeing all Partnership Notes (whoever they were written by) in draft, so as to try and

view them through the eyes of the Partners in order to anticipate their likely reaction.

A good leader is aware that hearts and minds are won by
communicating well. Sensitive and appropriate behaviour is
more powerful than an inspiring speech. What leaders should
never lose sight of is the importance of building personal and
team relationships with their people, as they are the company's
main assets.

The two greatest dangers a leader faces are:

1. to assume their title makes them a leader,

   and

2. to underestimate the importance of building a winning
   leadership team. A winning team needs to be cohesive and
   aligned; a group of talented individuals does not necessarily
   make a winning team.

The St. James's Place Leadership Team

The SJP leadership team has many talented individuals, but
the key to its success, reflected in the Company's growth from
launch in 1992 to a FTSE 100 company, is that every member
of the team:

❑ shares the same goals and vision

❑ has the same values and beliefs

❑ respects the different attributes and contributions that
   each team member brings to the party.

Each knows how their colleagues will react in certain circumstances and can anticipate what they might say.

The team comprises people who are themselves individual winners, many of whom could be the number one or chief executive in other companies. They choose, however, to remain as key members of a winning team – St. James's Place. The team members:

❏ lead by example

❏ are ambitious (for SJP as well as for themselves)

❏ are focused

❏ are determined to win

❏ never give up

❏ know their competitors

❏ hate losing

❏ learn from their mistakes

❏ are not complacent (always striving to improve).

They are well aware that their success as a leadership team is dependent on getting results through others in order to:

❏ win business

❏ win and retain talented people

❏ win support and followers

❏ win hearts and minds.

At St. James's Place **our assets are our people** and the leadership team knows that if we ever lose their hearts and minds we will be just like any other company.

KEY MESSAGES

YOUR TITLE DOESN'T MAKE YOU A LEADER
Followship and inspiring people does

- **Leadership is about:**
  - ➪ getting results through others
  - ➪ winning hearts and minds
  - ➪ leading and inspiring people to achieve the company's goals and vision
  - ➪ having the right attitude and being well-organised; self-discipline and resilience are essential
- **There are key differences between managing and leading**
- **The attributes of an effective leader:**
  - ➪ being authentic and trustworthy and leading by example
  - ➪ building strong relationships
  - ➪ exercising sound judgement and decision-making
  - ➪ communicating well
- **An effective leader asks questions, listens and 'hears what he doesn't want to hear'**
- **Common mistakes of a leader:**
  - ➪ lack of consistency between words and deeds, and not executing as promised
  - ➪ belief that an inspiring speech is more important than inspiring behaviour
  - ➪ assuming people will always make logical rather than emotional decisions
  - ➪ not stepping into the shoes of those around them and seeing through their eyes and perspective
  - ➪ **assuming their title makes them a leader**

CHAPTER 7

YOUR ASSETS ARE YOUR PEOPLE

If people are your assets treat them as such

UNFORTUNATELY, NOT EVERYONE THINKS like that. I remember a meeting in my office with a senior director of BAT shortly after they had acquired our financial services company, Allied Dunbar. The very high price they had paid almost entirely reflected the value of our people – in particular our sales force of around 4,500 at the time.

A phone call came through on my private line from our top salesman. I took the call, explained that I was in a meeting and would call him back.

The BAT director was clearly irritated by the interruption and asked who was calling me on my private line. I told him with pride that all the leading salespeople had my private line number and that the call was from John Ottensooser (the number one salesman) – pointing out to him that John was one of the most valuable assets BAT had just bought.

This annoyed him intensely, as he responded with the words:

'Don't tell me my friend what assets are – I'm the accountant, not you.'

I was not 'his friend'! And, clearly, not everyone agrees that people are their assets.

Effective leaders know that **people perform best** when they feel they are:

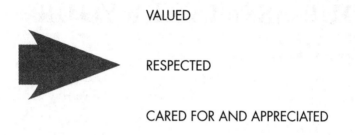

VALUED

RESPECTED

CARED FOR AND APPRECIATED

VALUED

A good starting point is to always treat people the way you want to be treated yourself. I always try to see things through the eyes of others.

An example is one-to-one meetings with my direct reports or top Partners at St. James's Place.

Seen through my eyes, any one of these meetings will be one of many during the month.

However, I try to remember that for each individual this will be their only meeting with me during the month. I feel I owe it to them to try to make the meeting as worthwhile as possible, which means looking through the notes I made at our previous meeting and preparing accordingly. I also try to ensure that the meeting starts on time.

I remember in the past my own preparation and antici-pation for what was an important monthly meeting for me with my boss. If my meeting was cancelled or rearranged I felt disappointed and let down. I reckoned that my meeting was clearly not that important to him. The same applied, but to a lesser extent, if my boss turned up late or if the meeting was delayed.

These were emotional reactions, I know, but when these things occurred, I did not feel particularly valued and I am sure that I would not be alone in feeling this. However, much as I regard being punctual as important, there are other ways of showing that you respect your colleagues.

Mark would be the first to say that time-keeping has never been one of his strengths. Hambro Life's charitable trust benefited from this when Mark would make a donation whenever he was late for a board meeting!

While this did not happen when he was late for a meeting with me, I never had the feeling of not being valued by Mark because he reassured me of this in other ways.

Mark always acknowledged my contribution in public at our annual conferences and to third parties (which I think he found easier to do than to my face!).

I also remember very well a charity auction at one of our Hambro Life dinners. We had just gone public, I had just been appointed to the board and the auction item I was after was the Hambro Life 'offer for sale' document signed by all the directors.

After some time Mark and I were left as the only bidders. I eventually withdrew, realising I could not afford to continue bidding and also because Mark started to make it clear he wanted me to!

I assumed, as the founder of Hambro Life, Mark quite understandably wanted the item for himself.

Despite having been pushed up on his bids by me, upon winning the auction he walked over and gave me the 'offer for sale' document, much to my delight.

This is a good illustration of a really effective leader motivating one of his people (me!). And it goes to prove that there are different ways of generating a sense of being valued in people other than turning up for one-to-one meetings on time!

RESPECTED

People respect those who show them respect.

It is important to treat everyone in your team as an equal and to recognise that each of them has as much to contribute as you do – just in a different way.

I am very aware (and so are they!) that I could not fulfil everyone's roles as well as they do. I could never be as welcoming as Myra on our switchboard, drive as well as John my driver, or be as successful a financial adviser as our leading Partners at St. James's Place. Equally, I think they would acknowledge that they could not do my job – there is mutual respect. Many people fall into the trap of feeling they should only show respect to their 'superiors' – but no one is superior to anyone else!

CARED FOR AND APPRECIATED

People do not perform well when they feel that they're being taken for granted. They perform at their best when they feel they are cared for and know that their contribution is really appreciated.

People who feel valued, respected, cared for and appreciated will not only up their performance, but also increase their loyalty to you and to their company.

It is a mistake to assume that your people are economic captives and that they will always make logical decisions based on financials rather than emotional decisions based on their feelings and how they are treated. I have heard too often that 'he or she won't leave', or 'they're not going anywhere' – a very dangerous assumption! Research commissioned by the insurance company Unum found that:

'Employees who feel cared for are 27% more likely to stay with their current employer for more than five years compared with those who feel only adequately or poorly looked after.'

If you subscribe to the view that your people are your assets, then their welfare should be high on your agenda.

For the first 10 years of J. Rothschild Assurance/St. James's Place, the second item on the agenda for directors' meetings – after previous minutes – was welfare of our people.

As the company grew, it necessitated moving to monthly reports to the board, setting out any individual welfare issues such as health or personal problems so that we could respond accordingly. This could be by sending cards, letters, flowers or by a phone call.

The most important time to show you care and appreciate your people is when they are going through tough times. It is when they need to know that you care more than ever. Congratulations letters when they are doing well will also be appreciated; though the recipients are feeling good, most people still do crave recognition. I remember making the mistake of dropping congratulations letters some time ago because I did not think it would be noticed, and on the basis that no one thanked me for them! I soon realised that I was wrong, and it hurt when people said that I was clearly less interested in how they were doing now that St. James's Place was so large. Some of them said how they kept all their congratulations letters in a separate file for posterity! I quickly reinstated the practice and have sent congratulations letters ever since!

There is a danger in all organisations of only recognising or acknowledging the top performers and excluding the solid, reliable performers who are often the backbone of your company. These people can easily be taken for granted as 'solid citizens' and not made to feel special – and yet these same people are often responsible for keeping the show on the road.

I have a TLC (tender loving care!) – rather corny, I know – on my daily action list to remind me to think of the less obvious people whom I should phone or send a thank you or well done message. I know that if it wasn't on my action list it would not happen. In the case of ill health or bereavement, I keep them on my action list because just contacting them on one occasion is insufficient.

As a leader, you should be caring and compassionate, but you will not be perceived as such by your people unless you actually show it. When you do, people will feel that they really are cared for and appreciated.

AND FINALLY: BE CONSTANTLY AWARE

An effective leader is aware and sensitive to the mood and morale of individuals in his or her team and how he can influence this. Leaders often develop their own network of advocates at all levels in their organisation upon whom they can rely for honest feedback on concerns and issues – before they surface. These people act as eyes and ears for the leader.

Your ability to sense the emotions of those around you is a valuable attribute.

The most junior person at a meeting will often feel insecure and less significant than others in the room. The leader should be aware of this and specifically ask the person for their views, making it clear how much they would be valued.

It is important to give credit to your people for their ideas. This gives them recognition and a feeling of self-worth. A leader should be aware of this, demonstrate humility and avoid the temptation to claim credit for themselves. I find that the use of the word **we** rather than **I** is good self-discipline. The message should be about 'the great team we have' – rather than about your own contribution.

An effective leader will step into the shoes of their people and see through their eyes and their perspective. He or she will be aware of the importance of praising people in public, and only ever reprimanding them in private.

The ability to be a chameleon at times is invaluable, and comes from being aware of the need to adjust to different people and adapt to the style of others.

I remember interviewing a potential finance director at St. James's Place. After a couple of interviews I asked him out to dinner and he asked whether he could bring his wife along, too.

I spent far too long at dinner reselling the potential finance director on the Company rather than focusing on his wife. I became aware – almost too late – that the decision was going to be hers and that he was already sold if she said yes. Fortunately she did, but I almost paid the price for my lack of awareness.

Effective leaders are constantly aware and sensitive to people around them, in particular to their people whom they have made an effort to get to know. They communicate well, exercise good judgement and ensure that their people feel valued, respected, cared for and appreciated. Through winning their hearts and minds they are able to inspire their people to perform exceptionally well in the pursuit of a common goal.

A good leader benefits from developing his or her people's potential by treating them at all times as the company's assets. If one of the valued assets leaves the company, the leader's first question should be 'where did **we** go wrong?' – rather than, as so often happens, implying the leaver is making a terrible mistake and that it is nothing to do with the company.

KEY MESSAGES

YOUR ASSETS ARE YOUR PEOPLE
If people are your assets treat them as such

- **People perform best when they feel that they are:**
  - ⇨ valued
  - ⇨ respected
  - ⇨ cared for and appreciated
- **Leaders need to be sensitive to the needs of their people:**
  - ⇨ see through the eyes of your people
  - ⇨ give credit to your people (not yourself)
- **Ask yourself: 'Where did we go wrong?'**
  - ⇨ if one of your valued assets leaves the company

CHAPTER 8

AVOID BEING 'ME TOO'

Differentiate yourself from the competition

THE KEY QUESTION TO ask yourself is: 'What is it that sets me or my business apart from my competitors and will persuade people to do business with me?'

Successful individuals or companies will make their case very compelling and they do this by differentiating themselves from the competition. They avoid being '**me too**'.

The same question should apply to your recruitment proposition: what differentiates you and will attract your key target recruits to join you?

When Mark and I had the original concept of forming a new financial services company in 1991, we knew that we had to be different in order to succeed in an already over-crowded marketplace. Our client proposition had to be different but also, very importantly, so did the proposition for our financial advisers and employees in order to attract them to join us.

What follows is not intended as a biography of JRA/SJP but to illustrate how we arrived at our three key differentiators and why, importantly, no single one is particularly original or clever but it's the combination of all three that works. This avoided us being perceived as 'me too' – or in this case another Allied Dunbar.

We decided that we would not only be the manufacturer of our products and services, but also the distributor by having our own dedicated team of advisers. We were often referred to as a 'virtual life company' because we, very unusually at the time, decided to contract out both our administration and investment management to the best in the field.

This allowed us to play to our management teams' strengths in product design, marketing and – most important of all – in distribution. We knew that the company would stand or fall on distribution – our ability to sell our products and services to our target audience.

'The Original Vision for J. Rothschild Assurance' in Chapter 2 describes how we undertook an audit of our competitors prior to launch and how we identified the 10 key attributes for JRA to be successful; those we called **Utopia Life**.

Of those key attributes, the three that differentiated us from others in our field were:

1. Our own team of experienced, high-quality advisers for distribution

Mark and I felt that we would be more in control of our destiny if we had our own distribution rather than having to compete for external distribution. We also had the advantage of actual experience in running our own distribution, unlike many others entering the field. We both believe in the benefits of focus and to do so solely on the needs of our own advisers appealed to both them and us.

Our distribution strategy was very different to that of our competitors. The majority of life assurance companies only marketed their products and services via IFAs. Some life companies had seen the advantage of building their own distribution network (sales force) in addition to relying on the IFA market, but had been largely unsuccessful.

In 1991, when we submitted our business plan to Tillinghast, the consulting actuaries, we were told that they were looking at six other business plans for life companies to build their own sales forces.

The common denominator among the other six 'me too' business plans was to build a sales force of a thousand advisers over five years. None of the six companies succeeded in doing so and not one of those sales forces exists today.

The defining characteristic of these almost identical 'me too' sales forces was recruiting people with no financial services experience, which inevitably resulted in:

❑ a high turnover resulting in a low retention rate of advisers

❑ low average adviser productivity

❑ poor public perception.

They all failed to create their own profitable distribution model – in other words, their models were flawed, particularly during a period of increased costs and regulation.

Our strategy was fundamentally different; we chose to ignore the IFA market altogether and to market our products and services exclusively via our own dedicated team of experienced, high-quality advisers. People had to 'qualify' to join J. Rothschild Assurance based on their previous experience and track record in financial services.

It became aspirational to join us – this was greatly helped by our having the name Rothschild and, unlike other companies in our field who called their people financial advisers, we differentiated our advisers by calling them Partners of the J. Rothschild Partnership.

Our strategy of only taking on experienced advisers eliminated the negative characteristics (just mentioned) of other sales forces. Our retention rate for advisers has been over 90% per annum, year in year out, and our average adviser productivity is around double the industry average.

Our new business is far more predictable than it would have been had we relied on the IFA market, because it is driven by the number of Partners (advisers) multiplied by their productivity. **We are more in control of our own destiny**.

The interests of SJP (as the provider) and of our Partners (as our distributors) are, uniquely, 100% aligned. They are:

❏ to grow and retain funds under management

❏ for SJP to build increased shareholder value

❏ for our Partners to build personal capital for the future. They can sell their practice in whole or in part, the value being based largely on their funds under management with SJP.

2. Our distinctive approach to investment management

This has enormous appeal to both our clients and our advisers. We had lost a few successful salespeople at Allied Dunbar to become IFAs purporting to be investment experts, which gave them enhanced status. As IFAs, they could offer their prospects and clients the choice of the investment universe rather than just Allied Dunbar's in-house investment management.

SJP's investment management proposition was also very different to that of our competitors. The typical life company (as with Allied Dunbar) had its own in-house investment department, which managed its policy holders' funds. Our strategy was to have our own funds but:

❏ to have no in-house fund managers, so avoiding any conflict of interest, and to contract out our investment management on a fee basis to external fund managers

❏ to have an Investment Committee – chaired by Mark for the first 20 years and advised by Stamford Associates (independent advisers).

The Investment Committee is responsible for selecting, monitoring and changing the individual fund managers as appropriate.

Our clients benefit because we can appoint the best fund managers in the world with wholesale purchasing power.

Our investment management strategy acknowledges that clients do not want to put all their eggs in one basket, should have geographical spread, and that no one investment manager or investment house has the monopoly of expertise. Our distinctive approach to investment management has given us a **competitive advantage** over other providers and financial advisers in the marketplace.

Our Partners have benefited enormously from our approach in acquiring clients and retaining funds under management. St. James's Place funds under management on our 25th anniversary in January 2017 were £75 billion.

3. The right culture

The third major differentiator for St. James's Place is our culture. It would be wrong to imply, despite our best endeavours, that new joiners buy into our culture from day one. Many are cynical, based on their past experiences working elsewhere. However, in time they do buy in, having experienced the SJP culture in practice.

I should emphasise that all the 10 key attributes identified at the outset for Utopia Life were essential for the Company to be successful and, indeed, remain so 25 years later.

The combination of the three attributes just covered still differentiate SJP today from others in our field and continue to give us competitive advantage.

Maintaining the right culture while being challenging with our growth is the most important attribute that we have.

If I leave a legacy I would like it to be the SJP culture rather than being remembered because my portrait is on the boardroom wall!

I will discuss the culture at SJP in more detail in Chapter 9.

I have used JRA/SJP as an example of a company avoiding being 'me too'. But **the same applies to individuals**. How do **they** avoid being 'me too' and so give themselves a competitive advantage over others in their company, who are their internal competitors, and over their external competitors in their marketplace? The answer lies largely in their personal brand.

The point so often missed is that not only companies such as Nike or Coca-Cola have brands – but so do individuals. We all have our own personal brand which defines our qualities, strengths and weaknesses; our individual brand values.

YOUR PERSONAL BRAND

A way to test your personal brand in business is to ask yourself how you think a client, a colleague, your boss or someone who works for you would describe you to an outsider.

WHAT ARE YOUR BRAND VALUES?

Different brand values will be important depending on your particular role in your organisation.

In a service business such as St. James's Place, our financial advisers are heavily dependent on introductions. A test for one of our advisers would be what they would like a client testimonial to say, or how they would like to be introduced to a prospective client.

WHAT MAKES YOUR BRAND VALUES DISTINCTIVE?

Our advisers would like to be described, I am sure, as:

❏ trustworthy, with their client's interests at heart

❏ having empathy and taking a genuine interest in their client and their client's aspirations for the future

❏ knowledgeable

❏ being patient and explaining things simply

❏ not over-promising and under-delivering

❏ not selling their client something today – never to be seen again.

These qualities would differentiate our advisers from the competition and allay the fears most people have – often based on their past experience – of dealing with financial advisers and financial institutions generally.

But, importantly, our advisers would also like their existing clients to say that they are likeable and a joy to deal with, and that, rather than dealing with some faceless institution, an SJP Partner takes personal responsibility to look after their clients and that:

❏ all phone calls are returned within 24 hours

❏ all correspondence is acknowledged within 48 hours

and that they are:

❏ reliable, efficient and accessible and always on time for appointments.

These last three qualities alone will differentiate them from most other financial advisers. It will almost certainly also differentiate them from other service providers such as the lawyers, accountants and banks that their clients deal with.

One very successful St. James's Place Partner underestimated the value of these particular qualities and paid the price for doing so.

I was at a dinner party when one of the guests sang the praises to everyone of St. James's Place and the advice that this particular Partner had given him on inheritance tax. I was delighted – until another guest asked for an introduction to this Partner. The client looked embarrassed and said that he would rather not make the introduction and suggested that I should recommend another Partner.

He went on to say that he was a friend of our Partner,

played golf with him and emphasised again how much he valued the advice he had received. He explained, however, that the problem was that the Partner was unreliable, totally disorganised, didn't return phone calls and frequently cancelled appointments or was late. For those reasons, he wouldn't recommend him.

Poor personal organisation had damaged a very successful and able Partner's personal brand in the eyes of his client. The price he paid was losing out on a new client who invested £500,000 through another Partner.

HOW TO IMPROVE YOUR PERSONAL BRAND

The majority of people rely on their company to help them to develop by putting them on various courses. In doing so, they are leaving it in someone else's hands as to when and if this should happen.

By being proactive ourselves we all have the opportunity to differentiate ourselves from competitors and to **develop ourselves on the job** (rather than in a classroom). This can be done daily to improve your personal brand.

How we perform in front of others will largely determine their perception of us. On the basis that I will be my own harshest critic, I continually rate myself at meetings or when giving talks.

I will rate my performance out of 10 after meetings, while it is still fresh in my mind. I assess:

❏ what did I handle well?

❏ what did I handle poorly?

And, importantly, my takeaway from this is:

❏ what will I do differently to improve my performance at future meetings?

This rating and personal assessment I apply after all meetings I attend – large, small or one-to-one. I do the same in respect of any talks or speeches I give. I will then amend my talk accordingly for the next time I give the same or a similar talk.

I am continually striving to be better at whatever I do – and I know that the time I cannot improve my personal performance and start rating myself 10 out of 10 is the day I should call it a day!

All people have a personal brand and those who are ambitious should continually strive to be better and to develop themselves if they want promotion and to climb the corporate ladder. I was one of those ambitious people!

Whenever I was attending a meeting (rather than running it), I would set aside enough time beforehand to study the agenda and any papers in depth. I would mark the papers based on the information I had as to what decision or conclusion I would come to if it were down to me, prior to any discussion.

At the same time, I would list any questions I had, or points I required further details on at the meeting, the answers to which could clearly change my preliminary views.

During the meeting itself I would test myself as to:

❏ whether I would have handled the discussions differently if I had been chairing the meeting

❏ whether all the attendees had been encouraged sufficiently to express their views

❑ whether I would have come to the same conclusions and final decisions as the chairman of the meeting if I'd been running it.

In other words, I would be looking at what I could learn from the meeting and the way it was run for the time when I would hopefully be the person running a similar meeting in the future!

THE WORLD DOESN'T STAND STILL

Today you or your company may have the edge over your competitors because you have successfully differentiated yourself, and you indeed may also have **first-mover advantage**. However, complacency is a disease to be avoided by individuals and companies. The world doesn't stand still. I firmly believe that if you stand still you will get left behind.

To stay ahead, you must focus not just on your own performance, but on those trying to beat you: your competitors.

Here are two examples of how SJP has kept ahead of the competition:

In 1992 we had started out as a life assurance company. The perception of life assurance companies and the competitive landscape changed over our first eight years. Because of this, in 2000, when Halifax took a 60% stake in us we rebranded ourselves and transformed ourselves into a wealth management company, adding banking and other services to our proposition. This was a tough decision to take as we knew in doing so we would almost certainly lose the power of having the Rothschild name because of other Rothschild companies already operating in this area. This indeed was the case and – after some initial fears – we rebranded ourselves as **St. James's Place Wealth Management**.

The other SJP example was some five years ago, when we saw that our potential market for the recruitment of only experienced financial advisers to join the SJP Partnership was both ageing (average age around 55) and shrinking dramatically. When we launched in 1992 the number of financial advisers working in the UK totalled quarter of a million. Today, thanks to increased regulation, there are only around twenty-five thousand – and yet it is acknowledged that there is a greater need for financial advice today than ever before. We saw this as an opportunity: there was an increasing demand for our services and less competition.

To capitalise on this, we made the decision to 'grow our own' and launched the **St. James's Place Academy**, in addition to continuing to recruit experienced advisers. There was one very important difference to what had been done previously by other companies: for the Academy, we only targeted people who were already successful in their particular fields but who wanted a change of career and way of life – so-called 'second careerists'.

The average age of Academy joiners is 38 – compared to 55 for the UK financial adviser population overall and 48 for St. James's Place. Of them, 22% are female – as opposed to only 10% in the wider market.

We now also run 'next-generation' Academy courses for sons and daughters of existing Partners, having detected a growing desire among our Partners to keep their practices in their family when they slow down or retire.

The innovation of the Academy once again gave us a competitive advantage and further differentiated SJP from other wealth management companies in our field.

The world doesn't stand still, and in order to win it's important to continually differentiate yourself and your company from your competitors – in other words to avoid being 'me too'.

SELLING IS NOT A DIRTY WORD!

How you or your company view selling will often make the difference between success, mediocrity or failure. It's a mistake to be 'me too' and to have the same view of selling as the majority of people – it could be a key differentiator for you.

In the fast-moving world in which we all live, what won't change is that all businesses and professions in whatever field have one thing in common: their goods and services must be sold for their business to survive.

Many professionals would not feel comfortable with the use of the word 'sold' because they have a narrow and negative view of selling. Few would view the ability to sell as a desirable attribute. Their definition of selling, at the extreme, might be something along the lines of:

'Manipulating people to buy something that they neither want nor need.'

That perception of selling is of unsolicited cold calls, aggressive sales techniques and the hard-sell often associated with double glazing, second-hand cars or financial scams. While there are undeniably some very undesirable sales practices, the majority of selling is conducted in a very different and acceptable manner.

I am aware that what follows may come across as **in defence of selling** – if so that's unintentional. My aim is to try to convince any doubters that the ability to sell is a major contributor to success for both individuals and businesses.

My own definition of selling is:

'The ability to persuade or convince people of the value, benefit and importance of what we offer.'

How many people would disagree that this is a desirable attribute?

I think that the point is often missed that the most

successful lawyers, barristers, accountants and surgeons (to name a few professions), while not having the word 'sales' on their visiting cards, often owe much of their success to their ability to sell. They are better than their competitors at persuading or convincing people of the benefit of taking their advice or using their services.

This was brought home to me at a dinner party where a well-known and successful plastic surgeon was one of the guests. He was charming and charismatic and the ladies were all captivated by him – much to my annoyance.

When the dinner was over and the plastic surgeon had left, our hostess described him as 'the best plastic surgeon in the country'. Having seen him operate – at the dinner table – I could understand why she described him as such. But there was no doubt in my mind that she had not based her judgement solely on his undoubted skills in the operating theatre, but also on his clear ability to **sell** or persuade and convince people that he was, indeed, the best. It was the combination of these attributes that had made him the most successful plastic surgeon in the country, which did not necessarily mean he was actually the best – although I am sure that he would dispute this!

Contrary to popular belief, many people actually benefit from someone else's ability to sell to them – in other words, from being sold to. I have never met a widow or widower who has complained that their husband was sold too much life assurance.

I could never sell anything that I didn't believe in and wouldn't buy myself were I in a similar situation. I believe that this applies to many people and the poor reputation of selling is brought about by those who are happy to sell anything to anyone – provided there are sufficient financial rewards for doing so.

Selling has been a major contributor to the success of St. James's Place over its 25 years in existence – as I am sure it has been for many businesses – and I am not just talking about the selling that SJP Partners do in this context. We have had to sell for a number of reasons.

1. To secure our original financial backing and to attract and retain our shareholders

In 1991 Mark and I had to sell or persuade Jacob Rothschild and Scottish Amicable as to why they should back us financially and, very importantly in the case of Jacob, to allow us to have the Rothschild name.

Today we still sell – but now to prospective and existing shareholders about why they should buy and retain our shares.

2. To recruit the founding members of the Company

We had to sell them on our vision for a new financial services company. We were always going to stand or fall on our ability to recruit the right leadership team, but also very importantly the right team of high-quality, experienced and successful financial advisers.

We had to persuade these key people to join us as founders and convince them that the value and benefit to them of joining us would far outweigh any short-term financial sacrifice they would suffer.

While it was clearly more challenging to recruit the key people we wanted as a start-up company, the challenge still exists today. Not only to recruit but just as importantly to retain key people.

No company can afford to be complacent in a very competitive world and St. James's Place is continually selling to our people on why being with SJP is the best place for them to thrive. We don't want to run the risk of a competitor successfully doing so.

3. To acquire and retain clients

Our Partners have to sell people on the value of their advice, our products and services in order to persuade them to become clients in the first place and, once they are, just as importantly to retain them as clients.

4. To gain support for the SJP Charitable Foundation

Joel Joffe persuaded Mark and I to create the charitable foundation from day one of the Company. He convinced us that the Company had a responsibility to the community and that management should encourage a culture throughout the business to 'give to those less fortunate than ourselves'.

Joel sold to us very effectively – although he would never have considered himself a salesman. He successfully **transferred his belief** to us.

I make no apology for saying that the Foundation is sold on a continuous basis within SJP because we believe it is a very important part of the St. James's Place culture to help the community.

Any leader is a salesman who has to sell to people inside and outside their company. Great leaders excel at selling their ideas and aspirations to others.

Jacob Rothschild (our original backer), our shareholders, our key people, our clients and the supporters of the St. James's Place Charitable Foundation all had to be successfully sold to. If they hadn't been persuaded as to the value, benefits and importance of what we were offering, we would either not be in business today or be a mediocre company in our field.

Selling in its many different forms and circumstances is a major contributor to the success of St. James's Place as it is for many successful companies.

KEY MESSAGES

AVOID BEING 'ME TOO'
Differentiate yourself from the competition

- **What will persuade people to do business with you?**
- **SJP's three key differentiators:**
  - ➪ our own team of experienced, high-quality advisers
  - ➪ our distinctive approach to investment management
  - ➪ the right culture
- **Everyone has a personal brand**
  - ➪ what's yours?
- **Your own self-development:**
  - ➪ develop yourself on the job – don't rely on your company
  - ➪ continually rate your own performance
  - ➪ what decision would you make in meetings if it were down to you?
  - ➪ how would you have run the meeting differently?
- **The world doesn't stand still**
  - ➪ avoid complacency – keep an eye on your competitors
  - ➪ keep ahead of the competition
  - ➪ gain competitive advantage
  - ➪ SJP started as a life assurance company – rebranded as a wealth management company
  - ➪ we founded the SJP Academy to grow our own advisers
- **A major contributor to success – the ability to sell**
  - ➪ doing the same things as others – but better – can be your differentiator

- ➪ selling is not 'manipulating people to buy something that they neither want nor need'
- ➪ selling is the ability to persuade or convince people of the value, benefit and importance of what you offer
- ➪ all businesses and professions have to sell their goods and services to survive.
- ➪ view selling as 'the transfer of belief'
- ➪ many people benefit from being sold to
- ➪ selling has been a major contributor to the success of St. James's Place
- ➪ great leaders excel at selling their ideas and aspirations to others

CHAPTER 9

THE RIGHT CULTURE

*The key to building a successful and
sustainable company*

MANY PEOPLE VIEW CULTURE as intangible. It may be hard to
articulate but, for me, culture is largely about people, their
collective behaviour and relationships. The right culture
comes from building appropriate habits in an organisation.

Most organisations have good intentions and a variety
of – often very well-written – statements setting out their
vision, mission, culture and values. Many use a similar set of
words and express similar sentiments. However, that is often
where the similarity ends.

The difference lies in how successful they are in putting the
words into practice. In the case of culture, the test is whether
the desired culture is truly embedded in the organisation so as
to become a part of its DNA. Published views alone can lead
to complacency and an assumption that they are actually lived
in practice when in fact they are not.

I would say that it is preferable not to have a written statement on culture and values – unless they are put into practice
day in and day out.

OWNERSHIP OF AND RESPONSIBILITY FOR CULTURE

Accountability for all aspects of culture rests with the chief executive and board. Their commitment has to be non-negotiable and they should be the role models and guardians of culture in their organisation. Their words on culture and values should be experienced by people in practice – **they should do as they say** – which will reinforce the authenticity of the leadership team.

It is therefore essential to ensure that all members of the leadership team (executive and non-executive) do actually have the same values and subscribe to the right culture.

While a board's responsibility extends to all areas of the business, it is important to have individuals on it who are focused on – and act as champions for – particular aspects of the business.

Broadly speaking, when recruiting non-executive directors, candidates are sought with particular skills in areas such as finance, legal and compliance. Surprisingly, I have never seen culture included. I think it should be. The chair should ensure that culture features as a regular topic on board agendas in the same way that, recently, diversity has. The chief executive is ultimately responsible for a company's culture, but when candidates are considered for that role, insufficient consideration is given as to whether a particular candidate is likely to maintain, enhance or destroy a company's culture.

The culture of successful companies that really believe their 'assets are their people' shows that people perform best when they feel respected, cared for and appreciated. In order to preserve that culture, it's essential that a new chief executive subscribes 100% to that view.

I believe that people generally treat others as they are treated themselves. If they feel that their organisation demonstrates integrity and openness in its dealings with them, they will mirror this in their own dealings with clients, suppliers, shareholders and regulators, as well as members of their community.

Many graduates and job applicants have told me how demoralising it is when they have applied for jobs and not had their application acknowledged and, even when it is, they often hear nothing further. The same applies to applications for funding from charitable trusts and foundations. This lack of courtesy and caring for people says a lot about an organisation's culture; the way it treats people externally is a reflection of how it treats its own people internally.

The right culture is essential in order to build a successful and sustainable company. It is therefore surprising that analysts very rarely comment on a company's culture when assessing its future prospects. Perhaps this is because they are trained to analyse numbers which they can put on their spreadsheets rather than cultures. So much of their focus is on forecasting short-term financial results rather than on the company's medium- to long-term future.

All too often, I have been told that having the right culture is easy for a start-up – but that it is virtually impossible to change the existing culture in a large, long-standing organisation, or to maintain or scale culture in one that is rapidly growing.

While it is undeniably harder, it is not impossible. The chief executive and board should not be defeatist, but should rise to the challenge, otherwise this view will become a self-fulfilling prophecy.

To look at the importance of culture, and the role it plays in the success of a company, I am going to focus on St. James's

Place – not only because I know it so well, but because, as it's grown from being a start-up 25 years ago into the substantial company it is today, it has had to face the challenge of maintaining its culture.

In the beginning, it was easy. We started in a small coach house in Cirencester, with a staff of three: my secretary Gail, my driver John and me. We were soon joined by David Bellamy, who started as head of operations and rose to became CEO of SJP. Even when we launched and moved into Dollar Street House with a larger staff, everyone was treated as equal, and mucked in and helped wherever they could; David used to pop out to the bakery opposite to buy buns for the staff. We used first names (as we do today), and there was an atmosphere of mutual respect and trust. This defined the culture of the Company from the beginning.

Today our total SJP community numbers over ten thousand – more than a bakery full of buns – including Partners, advisers, their support staff and SJP employees. We have offices all over the country, which range in size from one-man bands, to large practices, and to the hundreds who work at our Cirencester Head Office. Maintaining our culture through the rapid expansion has not been easy. Of our total community, three-and-a-half thousand are self-employed financial advisers (the Partnership), who operate in a highly regulated environment. While they are the key drivers of our business they also represent a significant potential risk. But the right culture should not be compliance-led. It isn't at SJP. What this risk means is that having the right culture is not just desirable for SJP; **it is vital**.

Trusted relationships are at the heart of our business and are based on how we do things, our behaviour and values. This applies equally between the Company and our people, and between our Partners and their clients.

There are aspects of our culture that have applied since our launch in January 1992, and still do today. I hasten to add that we are far from perfect. We inevitably fail at times to maintain different aspects of our culture – but we try to ensure that any inconsistencies are fed back to us by our people at all levels (not just managers) when they occur, in order to avoid any cultural drift. As with most companies we also obtain feedback from exit interviews and regular staff and client surveys.

We view our culture as a key differentiator for SJP but, more importantly, so do our people.

One of the highlights of a recent survey of the SJP Partnership was learning that:

'Partners overwhelmingly believe that the culture of SJP is a key differentiator.'

THE SJP CULTURE

I am sure that many successful companies in whatever field will have broadly similar features to SJP in terms of how they define their culture. They will, however, also have their own particular features depending on the nature of their business – and rightly so – in the same way that SJP's culture reflects the fact that we are in a people business.

We passionately believe that **our assets are our people** and we do our utmost to ensure that our people are not taken for granted but are treated as valued and trusted assets at all times.

Our culture very much reflects this. On their induction course, every new joiner is taught about these cornerstones of our culture:

We are a meritocracy: it is an individual's performance that counts, not their background or qualifications.

Respect has to be earned: management has to earn the respect of the Partnership and employees. Titles and stripes are irrelevant.

Mutual respect is key: respect must be two-way – upward and downward. Only then, we believe, can it be properly reciprocated.

No ivory tower: we do not have a separate suite of offices for directors, a directors' dining room or reserved car parking spaces based on status. People at every level have access to others at every level.

The Company is more important than any individual: self-interest is frowned on, as is personal gain at the expense of others. However able or successful an individual may be, they will not survive at SJP unless they subscribe to our values.

Constructive criticism is encouraged: we aim to listen to – not talk at – our people, because we do want to hear what we don't want to hear. We will always strive to be better and recognise the danger of complacency. We encourage people at every level to put their head above the parapet and to make suggestions and constructive criticism **internally.** At the same time, our people will quickly close ranks when criticism of SJP occurs **externally.**

A 'can do' mentality: this is instilled in all our people, who will always explore alternatives to see how something can be done.

Under-promise, over-deliver: our aim is to be different to others who often over-promise and under-deliver.

24-hour phone back: we commit to returning calls within 24 hours, or the same day whenever possible.

We strive to ensure that we have good and trusted relationships with all our stakeholders: we care about and respect not only our internal community but – very importantly – our clients, suppliers, shareholders, our regulator and those in the wider community.

The points I have listed above are largely about SJP's internal culture: how we treat one another. But our culture extends to how we treat people outside the Company. This is as important to the success of our business as it is to the image we project to the wider world.

This external culture can be summed up by the following:

❏ We strive to exceed the expectations of our clients and avoid hiding behind the small print.

❏ We ensure our suppliers are treated fairly and paid on time.

❑ We aim to give our shareholders above-average growth in our share price.

❑ We are open with our regulator.

❑ The community benefits through the St. James's Place Charitable Foundation and all our staff receive two days a year to give to community support.

Culture is often seen as merely flowery words or vague promises. We recognise that and know that actions speak louder than words, and it is for this reason that we endeavour to make our culture tangible where possible.

CARING FOR THE COMMUNITY

The St. James's Place Charitable Foundation:

Around 90% of our people currently give monthly from their earnings in addition to participating in and supporting numerous fundraising events.

ACCESSIBILITY OF MANAGEMENT

The SJP Welfare List:

Our management teams in the offices around the country are responsible for feeding into the centre any health or personal problems that their people may have so that we can help in any way we can. This forms our Welfare List which is updated monthly.

I now have one real worry about our list which is how few of our people are reported as having mental health problems.

I would, of course, be delighted if I felt this were actually the case.

In a recent publication commissioned by the Government, *Thriving at Work*, the Stevenson/Farmer review points out that in any organisation the vast majority of people will have first-hand experience of mental health problems and a quarter will have experienced mental health issues themselves.

SJP can't be any different.

I'm sure that SJP will adopt the mental health core standards set out in the excellent executive summary of *Thriving at Work*. It would be remiss not to do so.

CARING FOR OUR PEOPLE

Our 'No Hiding Place' Document:

Everyone at SJP has a No Hiding Place document which lists directors' and senior managers' private line numbers, mobile/home phone numbers and email addresses, and this information is also published on the intranet. Any of our people can feel free to contact them directly. It's been that way since day one. Once, the chief executive of one of our competitors asked me to confirm that it was true about our No Hiding Place document. I told him it was and he was amazed and went on to say that he wouldn't allow any of his salespeople to have his direct office line, let alone his home number. But, in 25 years, I have probably only had two calls at home from SJP people that haven't been absolutely necessary. I truly believe that, if people know you are available, they will not take advantage of such privileges.

There has been, until very recently, one major omission in our SJP culture and I hold myself accountable since we never addressed it when we launched the Company. We were so focused on recruiting people to join us that we didn't think about how we should look after and show how we valued the contribution of our retirees. We never set up a system to stay in touch with them – by putting them on the distribution list for a newsletter from time to time, including then in SJP Foundation matters as well as inviting them to certain events. Other companies would outshine SJP in this respect – despite our culture being built around a people business. This has now been addressed.

A HEALTHY COMPANY CULTURE

Our experience shows that happy Partners and employees – and now hopefully happy retirees – lead to happy clients who will recommend SJP to others.

The two key indicators of a healthy company culture that we monitor most closely are:

❏ the retention rate of our people

❏ the retention rate of our clients and their funds under management.

We firmly believe that our culture gives us a competitive advantage and is unique – although I do accept that is a much-abused word.

The next chapter, **The Best Kept Secret** is about the SJP Charitable Foundation, which is viewed by our own people as the major contributor to our culture.

KEY MESSAGES

THE RIGHT CULTURE
The key to building a successful and sustainable company

- Culture is largely about people, their collective behaviour and relationships
- The right culture comes from building appropriate habits in an organisation
- It is dangerous to assume that written words are lived in practice
- It is preferable not to have a written statement on culture and values if they are not lived day in and day out
- Ownership and responsibility for culture lies with the chief executive and board
- Culture should feature as a regular item on board agendas
- Consider when appointing a chief executive whether they are likely to maintain, enhance or destroy a company's culture
- The way an organisation treats people externally is often a reflection of how it treats its own people
- SJP Partners 'overwhelmingly believe that the culture of SJP is a key differentiator for the business'
- SJP strives to have a good and trusted relationship with all our stakeholders:
  - ➪ clients
  - ➪ suppliers
  - ➪ shareholders
  - ➪ regulator
  - ➪ community

- **SJP endeavours to demonstrate our commitment to having the right culture:**
  - ⇨ caring for the community – **SJP Charitable Foundation**
  - ⇨ caring for our people (and retirees) – **Welfare List**
  - ⇨ accessibility of management – **Our 'No Hiding Place' document**
- **SJP believes our culture gives us a competitive advantage**
  - ⇨ embedded in the organisation and part of the Company's DNA
- **The right culture is essential in order to build a successful and sustainable company**

CHAPTER 10

THE BEST KEPT SECRET

*The hidden benefits of **workplace** and **personal** charitable giving*

I HAVE SAVED THIS chapter on charitable giving for last – not because it is the least important, but because in many ways I believe it to be the **most important**, certainly among the **most worthwhile** areas to which a company – and an individual – can devote time and energy. And if you truly want to be CEO of your life, I believe that you need to think of charitable giving as an integral part of your life and as a form of achievement in itself.

While growing an organisation there are so many things to think about: generating business, of course, complying with regulations, creating and maintaining a culture so as to keep employees, clients and investors happy and productive. All these factors remain important as an organisation matures, and can keep those at the helm occupied for more than there are hours in a day.

However, I believe that for a concern to be truly successful, it needs to be more than a profit-generating machine; it has to **give back**. But, what is most surprising – and why this chapter is titled *The Best Kept Secret* – is that **by giving you get so much more than you may expect in return**.

Throughout this book I have used St. James's Place as an example – mainly because it is the company I know best, and with which I have been most involved in every aspect from its genesis to where it is now – but in this chapter I make no apologies for concentrating on SJP. Quite simply, it is doing workplace giving better than any other company in this country (as far as I know).

The Government agrees. **In its 2011 Giving White Paper, St. James's Place was featured as the only case study on best practice in workplace giving.**

THE ST. JAMES'S PLACE CHARITABLE FOUNDATION: HOW IT ALL BEGAN

The Foundation was included as part of the Company's five-year vision statement at our launch in 1992:

> *'A charitable foundation supported by our people
> to give back to those less fortunate than ourselves.'*

Joel Joffe – who was a member of Nelson Mandela's defence team in South Africa before he came to London and joined Mark at Abbey Life – should have the credit for persuading Mark and me to create the SJP Charitable Foundation (originally J. Rothschild Assurance Foundation) from day one. Joel convinced us that we should not only focus on a public floatation for the Company after five years and on making money for our shareholders and ourselves, but that the Company had a responsibility to the community and that the management team should encourage a culture throughout the business to give to those less fortunate than themselves.

Every person joining the Company was – and still is – told about the Foundation on their induction course and given the chance to sign a covenant, dedicating a pre-determined amount from their monthly earnings to charity. In the first year, £17,000 was raised from covenants and events. But, as the years passed, and as the Foundation became more organised and professional, so it became more deeply embedded in the DNA of the Company.

HOW SJP AND OUR DONORS BENEFIT FROM THE FOUNDATION

What we did not anticipate at the time was that there would be significant additional benefits to SJP as a company from creating the Foundation. These, while not always tangible, possibly exceed the warm feeling we all get from making a positive and lasting difference to other people's lives. It is not only the beneficiaries of our giving who benefit; SJP itself, and our donors, benefit enormously.

At SJP, the Foundation is the major contributor to our unique culture. It is our Best Kept Secret.

In a recent survey of our people, no other single factor was rated higher:

❑ **95%** of the community felt that our Foundation was **essential** or **very important** to the **SJP culture**

❑ **20%** felt that it was the **key** factor in enhancing the Company's culture.

We found that, if the lead comes from the top and a company's foundation is promoted strongly, it will create a tremendous sense of pride and achievement – and that giving will become part of a company's culture and lead to a **feel-good factor** and a **positive, happy and cohesive workforce**.

Benita Refson, CBE, the founder of the wonderful charity Place2Be, having spoken at our City office described the SJP audience as:

> *'The most engaging and receptive audience I have addressed.'*

MEASURING CULTURE THROUGH CHARITY

I make no apologies for returning to the subject of culture. Having the right culture should be a key objective for all organisations. But because it is difficult to measure, culture is unlikely to feature as one of the company's KPIs (key performance indicators). However, the major contributor to a company's culture – at least in SJP's case – can be measured by the KPI for the company's charitable trust, which should be included in the annual business plan like any other targets or key objectives.

At SJP, the Foundation's board sets objectives, which are included in our business plan, as for any other major aspect of our business.

Targets and KPIs are set for:

1. Funds raised
- total amount to be raised during the year
- % of community donating by monthly covenant
- average amount of monthly donation.

2. Funds donated

- total amount donated during the year
- % split between UK and overseas causes
- amount donated by way of large and small grants as well as by local office allowance grants.

Progress against all these targets and KPIs is included in the monthly statistics pack for the Foundation.

Appropriate monthly management information ensures that new Partners and employees are asked whether they would like to contribute to the Foundation on a monthly basis and whether (say) the processing of grants is operating efficiently.

LEAD FROM THE TOP

A number of years ago, Joel Joffe (as chairman) and I were on the committee of the Giving Campaign (a Government initiative to increase company giving).

We arranged meetings with the chief executives of many of the largest UK companies, in order to encourage them to promote, in particular, payroll-giving among their workforce. All too often their response was: 'I'll certainly have a word with our HR people about promoting payroll-giving more actively.'

Unsurprisingly, when we followed up to see how successful this had been – whether the take-up rate had increased – little had changed.

For a company's foundation to be successful and to secure buy-in from its people – **the lead must come from the top**.

The chief executive, chairman and the board need to be seen to be 100% committed to the foundation by supporting it in every way possible, not only financially on a personal basis but also by devoting their time to attend and participate in fundraising events. This is not only good for morale, but it's fun, too. Though you may have to choose how you support any events: I enjoy a backgammon tournament rather more than a triathlon (though I also get a kick from greeting the runners at the finishing line)!

COMPANY MATCHING ALL MONEY RAISED

The directors of SJP decided from day one that the Company would make contributions to the Foundation when it was in a financial position to do so. In 1999 the Company was able to honour its commitment with shareholder approval by matching all money raised.

The obvious appeal of every pound donated being doubled by the Company added great impetus to our fundraising.

FROM LITTLE ACORNS . . .

One of our first big charity partners came about by chance. For the first five years, SJP had concentrated on British-based charities. But, in 1999, the Foundation's board decided to cast the net wider and gave Gail Mitchell-Briggs, then my PA, the task of finding suitable charities that worked abroad. She was reading through a magazine when she spotted an advert appealing for donations to a – then small – charity called Hope and Homes for Children. When she got home, she called the number on the advert and spoke to Caroline Cook, one half of the husband-and-wife team who founded it. Caroline told Gail that, by happy chance, her husband, Colonel Mark Cook, was going to be on TV as the subject of that night's episode of *This is Your Life*.

A few days later, Gail called the Cooks to say that the Foundation board would like to meet them. The rest has gone down in SJP history. Since 1999, the Foundation has given over £7 million to Hope and Homes for Children and helped to lift it from being a small charity with big aims, to being one of the most important and effective advocates in the field.

But this is where the other half of the equation fits in: Mark Cook regularly invited members of the SJP community – those who had done most to support the charity – on trips to see what they were doing in the field. I was privileged to go to Ukraine with two Partners. The day we arrived, we were taken straight to a state orphanage. It was heart-breaking. It was as if the children were in a battery farm. They looked at us with dead eyes, and they didn't cry. When I asked the person running the orphanage why it was so silent, I was told it was because the children knew that no one was listening.

We went back to the hotel feeling depressed. But the next day was a revelation. Hope and Homes takes children out of orphanages and places them in real homes – with their wider family or foster parents. We were taken to one of these homes, where a couple of lawyers had given up their work to look after children who had been in the orphanage. There was light in their eyes. It was such a happy scene – there was no way that anyone who saw this could help but support the charity. It gave us a huge sense of pride and achievement – as well as a deeper perspective on life.

It is only one of **hundreds of charities**, big and small, that the Foundation has supported over the last 25 years. Most have involved children, hospices and charities helping people with cancer – the causes picked by our community to focus on.

CLEAR ACCOUNTABILITY, ROLES AND RESPONSIBILITIES

One of the secrets to the SJP Charitable Foundation's success is that it is run with the same seriousness and professionalism as other areas of the business. It has a board of trustees (which include the four executive directors of SJP); a Foundation committee, with a representative from every SJP office; a Foundation office, which carries out the day-to-day activities of the Foundation, and ambassadors, who come from the wider community of wives, husbands or partners of Partners, directors or employees, and who help the Foundation office to vet charities applying for funds and monitor those charities that have received funds to ensure that the appropriate outcomes have been achieved.

FUNDS FOR OUR FOUNDATION COME FROM TWO MAIN SOURCES

Our own community

Members of the Partnership and employees – as well as our wider community, which includes our fund managers, suppliers and service centres. They often generously support the Foundation by sponsoring events or taking tables at our fundraising events.

The Company

With shareholder approval, matching pound-for-pound all money raised each year.

MONTHLY DONATIONS

Of the people who joined SJP before 2015, **92% donate monthly by deed of covenant** with an average monthly contribution of £35. To put this into context, the average of similar companies is around 10% of employees. Monthly covenants (including matching and Gift Aid) account for approximately 40% of the total funds raised each year.

FUNDRAISING EVENTS

The balance of money raised each year comes from numerous fundraising events organised by Partners and employees, putting the 'fun' into fundraising.

These range from fun events such as:

❑ quiz evenings

❑ raffles of theatre, football, rugby tickets, etc.

❑ race nights

❑ boxing evenings

❑ cake sales

❑ Britain's (or St. James's Place's Got Talent-style shows

❑ dinners and balls

to the 'less fun' – at least from where I'm sitting (comfortably) such as:

❑ five-a-side football competitions

❑ endurance walks

❑ marathons (London, New York, Sahara and the Jungle Marathon)

❑ triathlons

❑ annual cycle ride

❑ climbing mountains (including Everest!).

People at all levels and in different parts of SJP participate in all manner of events – which is great for team-building and morale. Whatever their rank or position in the Company, they are equal on the Foundation pitch, and united in their aim of raising as much money as possible for charity.

The Company organises rather more formal money-raising opportunities. These include a raffle at the Annual Company Meeting (ACM) and the Annual Company Dinner and overseas conference dinners.

On these occasions a speaker, often a recipient of funds from the Foundation, comes in person to thank the Company for its support and to appeal for further contributions from the attendees. There are pledge forms on the dinner tables offering individuals the opportunity to give a one-off donation or to increase their monthly covenant. They can and often do both! Perhaps unsurprisingly, the more wine that's drunk, the more generous they become (another good reason to ensure that good wine is flowing freely). No one who was there will forget the time that Stephen Sutton spoke at the ACM. He was a young man with cancer. When he was told that it was terminal, he set himself a target: to raise £10,000 for the Teenage Cancer Trust. SJP promised him a donation to speak at the ACM. He talked about his situation with such positivity and about the bucket list of things he wanted to do before he died. It was electrifying and captured the admiration of everyone present. That evening, he and his mother came to the dinner for the top-performing Partners. When he stood up to thank everyone for the £5,000 donation, the effect was extraordinary. People started pledging more and more. In the course of that day and evening he raised £388,000 (including Company matching) for the Teenage Cancer Trust. A further £128,000 rolled in after that event meaning that through the generosity of our community of givers over half a million pounds was donated, helping him reach his first £1million. Stephen died prematurely, aged 19, in 2014, but his story has continued to raise money for the Teenage Cancer Trust: the total, in February 2018, stood at £4,961,257.

I have never subscribed to the often-expressed view that people will either give by monthly deed of covenant or will participate in or sponsor fundraising events – but not both.

There is no evidence of this at SJP – just the opposite. Some people don't think much about giving, but somehow – in whatever form – it becomes part of their DNA once they become part of SJP. I'm not sure giving was in mine until I met Joel Joffe. But it seems that it's contagious: being in a community of givers instils a desire to give in people who have not previously done so.

WHERE DOES THE MONEY GO?

As important as it is to raise money, it is vital to ensure that the fruits of people's generosity go to deserving causes. At SJP, the community is involved in choosing the general areas to which we direct our giving. We have chosen to:

❏ support small and medium-sized charities where our grant can really make a difference

❏ give priority to those charities where our own people are involved or are making a major contribution. Two of our Partners, for instance, have founded their own brilliant charity, setting up youth centres in Nepal, to which the Foundation has contributed (though it was judged on its own merits!)

❏ match funds raised and cover the administrative expenses, overheads and staff costs of the Foundation, so that all money raised can be donated to the causes the Foundation supports.

It's impossible, here, to do justice to the Foundation and to the incredible charities with which it has been involved, and to the community members who have given both cash and time. For example, one wonderful member of our Nottingham office, for his 60th birthday, invited friends and colleagues to join him on a Saturday, in building a courtyard for underprivileged children to play in.

EVERYONE WINS

Do not underestimate the importance of recognising people's generosity. At SJP, all offices where over 90% of their people donate monthly are shown on the screen at the Annual Meeting each year, and there is an annual award given to the person who has made an outstanding contribution to the Foundation.

While certainly not the motive behind having the Foundation, there is no doubt that a by-product is that **SJP clients like being with a company that gives something back to society**. We have, however, never used the Foundation as a marketing tool nor sought publicity. If we happen to receive publicity because a recipient puts out a press release to gain local coverage – all well and good.

The St. James's Place Charitable Foundation is increasingly acknowledged as one of the most successful charitable foundations in the corporate sector and a role model for other companies to emulate.

By SJP's 25th birthday in January 2017, it had given an extraordinary £55 million to 775 different charities. In 2016 alone, the SJP Foundation raised £7.6 million.

SOME QUOTES FROM THE 2016 FOUNDATION SURVEY

'I have recently joined SJP but the enthusiasm and vigour with which the Foundation is presented and supported is a real positive for the feel of SJP and makes me even more proud to work here.'

'As a Partner who joined in 2015, the Foundation, and the way it demonstrates the values of SJP, was a key element behind my decision to join. Already I am very proud of it and understand why so many within the family are passionate about it.'

'The Foundation is the absolute heart of SJP and something I am immensely proud of.'

'I am incredibly proud to work for a company with such a strong charitable giving side. The Foundation demonstrates the compassionate, caring and giving side of the Partners and employees.'

One participant described the Foundation as:

'The jewel in SJP's crown.'

These quotes confirm my passionate belief that workplace charitable giving is great for business and for creating a positive culture within a company; done right, it can be the **glue that binds a workforce together**. While I do believe it's been our best kept secret, I do not believe that it should be a secret if it encourages more charitable giving in the corporate sector.

THE HIDDEN BENEFITS OF PERSONAL CHARITABLE GIVING

The personal benefits from charitable giving are immeasurable.

A meaningful, ongoing commitment to charitable giving not only makes a positive and lasting difference to other people's lives but, very importantly, to our own lives as well. It really is one of those rare win-win situations.

Could I Live on 99% of My Income?

Very few people would disagree that all of us should give to those less fortunate than ourselves – assuming, of course, that we are in a financial position to do so. Nevertheless, it is estimated that, despite the generous tax incentives, people only donate on average less than 1% of their total income to charity each year, with higher income earners donating a smaller percentage of their income to charity than the less well paid.

How many of us could, honestly, answer, no – that we could not live on 99% of our income or that it would have an adverse effect on our standard of living?

There's enormous potential to increase the average percentage donated per individual if they could be persuaded as to how they could dramatically improve the lives of many people and, through doing so, also make their own lives more rewarding.

My Own Experience

I do not think that I would be alone in saying that, for much of my life, my own personal charitable giving was not meaningful, and often reactive and sporadic. I gave mainly in response to sponsorship requests from friends or work colleagues participating in events such as the London Marathon, and by accepting the occasional invitation to a charity ball or dinner. I had never contemplated setting aside any particular amount of money each year to give away – although I could have easily afforded to have done so.

I do not think it was because I was a particularly mean person, but charitable giving just had not been high on my agenda as I focused on progressing my career to the exclusion of almost everything else.

Additionally, there is a tendency in most of us – and I count myself in this group – to turn a blind eye to the plight of others, not because we do not care but because it disturbs us and makes us feel uncomfortable. It is ironic that those are two of the main reasons we should lend our support.

What Changed My Attitude to Charitable Giving?

It was when I realised that an important attribute of a good business leader was to hear what I did not want to hear. I then realised that equally applied to other aspects of my life and that I should get out of my comfort zone and seek to see and hear about those considerably less fortunate than myself. I did find many of my visits to charities disturbing and emotionally draining – but that was the motivation for me to try to make a difference. Seeing convinced me. It was because of this that I put charitable giving high on my agenda; the ideal vehicle for me to facilitate this at the time was through my previous company, Hambro Life/Allied Dunbar's charitable trust.

The Joy of Giving

At the same time as donating on a monthly basis to the Company's charitable trust, I opened a CAF (Charities Aid Foundation) account and donated a fixed amount each year into that account. CAF provide me with a cheque book which enables me to support particular charities of my choice and to continue to respond to individual requests from participants in various charitable events. There is the added benefit of the attractive tax advantages of Gift Aid applying so it is a very tax-efficient way of giving to charity.

I like the idea that I can determine in advance how much I will give to charity each year both through my monthly contributions to the St. James's Place Foundation and to my CAF account.

My Own Charitable Trust

In the same way that forming the Foundation was one of the best business decisions we made as a company, starting my own charitable trust was one of my best personal decisions. Again, Joel Joffe deserves the credit for this.

Having persuaded Mark and myself to create the St. James's Place Charitable Foundation (originally the J. Rothschild Assurance Foundation), he persuaded both of us to form our own charitable trusts. Joel subtly raised the topic by saying that he didn't think either of us was particularly mean and that he thought we were both charitably minded. He went on to say that, if the company we were launching turned out to be as successful as we hoped it would be, he was sure we would each give generously to charity. He suggested that we would probably be relaxed about eventually donating around 10% of the value of our own founder shares at the time. Neither of us disagreed.

Simple and Less Painful

Joel suggested that we would find it far simpler and, in his words, 'less painful' to make the decision today, when our shares only had a nominal value, rather than wait for the Company – hopefully – to go public. He persuaded us to form our own charitable trusts (even recommending the firm of lawyers we should use!) and that we should each put 10% of our founder shares into the trusts straight away.

Mark and I both took the point that making the decision at that time was easier than disagreeing with Joel's logic and each of us having to write a cheque sometime in the future for, say, over £1million depending of course on the future value of our shares.

Founder Shares

The idea of doing this is so simple that I am sure that the majority of people starting companies would be receptive to doing the same thing. The timing of doing so before the company has any real value is ideal, when your view of its possible future value is based on hope and cannot be accurately determined. There is no downside because, if your company unfortunately fails, then the cost to you (and others with founder shares) of each having put, say, 10% of your shares into personal charitable trusts has been nothing.

Assuming the aspirations you have for your company materialise, the advantage is that you made the irrevocable decision some years ago as to how much of your newly acquired wealth you would donate to charity.

If you are in the fortunate position of being able to form your own charitable trust funded by regular donations, or through putting some of your assets such as shares into the trust, it really is worth considering. Because the trust's assets are no longer yours, the only decisions you have to make in the future are which charities you wish to support.

Additional Benefits from Having My Own Charitable Trust

Although it was not an influencing factor at the time of starting my own charitable trust, I do like the idea of leaving this as a legacy to my daughter and grandchildren. My daughter, Panda, and my partner, Sophie, are, with me, trustees of the trust. We will allow the grandchildren to decide every year to which charity (or charities) they would each like £1,000 to go. This will hopefully make them aware (at a far earlier stage in their lives than their grandfather) how they can help people considerably less fortunate than themselves.

CHARITY AS AN INVESTMENT

I now view charitable giving in the same way as any other investments I may make.

Due Diligence

I find out as much as I can about any charity that I am thinking of investing in. I look at their track record, read their report and accounts, discover who is running the charity and who their trustees are. In the case of larger investments, I also like to visit the charity. My main interest is in how any money I give will be used: will it make a difference, and what is the targeted outcome? In other words, I am looking for a return on my investment (sometimes in the long term, as in the case of research). This is no different to when I am investing in a pension or ISA and, as in the case of these two investments, the tax advantages give further incentive to invest.

During our life, most of us aspire to building pots of money for our own good and future needs – perhaps in retirement. We will channel our money often on an annual or monthly basis into pensions, ISAs or unit trusts.

At the same time as taking care of our own needs, should we not also encourage people to care for the needs of others far less fortunate than ourselves and to build a fourth pot of money for their benefit?

Wills and Legacies
Many people generously leave money to charity in their wills, and legacies are a major source of income for charities. These people presumably often feel that their heirs will be inheriting enough anyway. I feel having 'enough' equally applies to many of us while we are still alive and is the reason for encouraging people to set aside an amount of money for their charity investments as naturally – and as regularly – as they do for their ISAs, pensions and savings.

The Unsung Heroes
Recognition is frequently given to those who donate significant sums to charitable causes – and rightly so. However, the unsung heroes are often:

❑ those who donate smaller amounts which nevertheless represent a large percent of their total discretionary spend, and also:

❏ the many people who volunteer their time for charitable causes. They are also making a significant investment of enormous value to charities. In many cases this is as great a personal commitment as donating money.

The financial reward for success in business is often an anti-climax, but it need not be if you take advantage of the choice money gives you and invest generously in charitable causes. Your investment, whether it is time or money, is personally rewarding.

I now firmly believe that you can get all you need or want in life if you help others get what they need or want.

The hidden benefits of personal charitable giving are often only really appreciated when you actually experience them, and that is probably why, as with workplace charitable giving, it remains the best kept secret.

But it shouldn't be.

KEY MESSAGES

THE BEST KEPT SECRET
*The hidden benefits of **workplace** and **personal** charitable giving*

Workplace Charitable Giving
- **The key factor in enhancing SJP's culture is the Charitable Foundation**
- **It's not only the beneficiaries who benefit from the Foundation – SJP itself and our donors benefit enormously. It really is win-win**
- **The six keys to success – embedding the Foundation in SJP's culture and DNA:**
  - ⇨ lead from the top
  - ⇨ Company matches all money raised
  - ⇨ part of the Company's vision and business plan
  - ⇨ clear accountability, roles and responsibilities
  - ⇨ ownership within the community (the donors)
  - ⇨ strong internal marketing and communications
- **SJP vision statement:**
  - ⇨ giving back and helping those less fortunate than ourselves. The Foundation should be embedded in the SJP culture, with the widest possible membership of the SJP community inspired to give both time and money to the Foundation

Personal Charitable Giving
- **Could I live on 99% of my income?**
- **Tendency in all of us to turn a blind eye to the plight of others because it disturbs us and makes us feel uncomfortable**
- **Monthly giving is painless**
- **Own charitable trust:**
  - ⇨ founder shares – no downside
  - ⇨ assets no longer yours so only decision is which charities to support
  - ⇨ legacy for children, grandchildren
- **View charity as an investment:**
  - ⇨ like any other you make
- **You get all you want in life if you help others get what they need or want**

ACKNOWLEDGEMENTS

THERE ARE TWO GROUPS of people whose help has been invaluable to me: those who have specifically helped with the book
itself and whose advice and guidance throughout I appreciate enormously, and the many people who have had a major
influence on my life and on the way I am – much of which is
reflected in the book. Several fall into both categories.

For the book itself, thank you to:

Mark Weinberg, who initiated the idea, encouraged me
throughout and helped me with ideas and suggestions from
start to finish.

Samantha Weinberg (Mark's daughter) has been a key
player in the process. She has done a brilliant job in convey-
ing what I was struggling to say, nudging it from something
resembling a best-practice guide or manual to a more personal
book based on examples drawn from my own experiences. In
addition, Sam was persuaded to take responsibility for whatever needed to be done to ensure that there was a finished
article. Without Sam, I don't believe the book would have ever
seen the light of day.

John Bond and Caroline McArthur at Whitefox Publishing
who, with professionalism and sensitivity, made everything
easy for us at the pointed end of publishing, and are responsible

for the many technical processes required to turn the manuscript into the book.

My reader/advisory group, whose contribution has been invaluable: Dennis Stevenson, the late Joel Joffe, Chris Woodhams, David Penney, Bob Cowell and, last but certainly not least, Elizabeth Downie, my secretary, who somehow succeeded in deciphering my numerous handwritten drafts.

Credit for sales and distribution of the book (with proceeds going to the St. James's Place Charitable Foundation) go to the quickly assembled 'St. James's Place Book Sales Team' of Sonia Gravestock, Malcolm Cooper-Smith and Mark Longbottom, ably led by Ian Gascoigne.

Sophie and my daughter, Panda, who encouraged me to keep going and not to give up.

To the people who have had a major influence on my life, thank you to:

Jacob Rothschild, for backing Mark and myself and trusting us with the Rothschild name to launch J. Rothschild Assurance (later to become St. James's Place).

Syd Lipworth, who, with Mark Weinberg and Joel Joffe, had a major influence on my business life at Hambro Life/ Allied Dunbar.

Finally, I am not going to list by name the numerous other people who have had a major influence on – and contributed to – my life generally. In addition to some very good personal friends, I am referring to work colleagues over the years – both past and present. I really could not have wished to work with a more interesting, loyal, fun and diverse group of individuals whom I view as part of my extended family.

I have been very lucky.

London, January 2018

Comments from colleagues at St. James's Place Wealth Management:

'During my 30 years in the City I have yet to meet a more accomplished and inspirational entrepreneur. If, like me, you tend to avoid books that will apparently teach you something, make this your exception.'

Jeremy Barrett

'A few minutes with Mike Wilson will change your life and I am truly grateful to him for changing mine.'

Gay Worrow

'Mike is the best people person I have ever met, who not only cares about the businesses he has established and grown, but also the people in them – most of whom would follow him anywhere!'

Paul Rothwell

'I could write a book about Mike Wilson's attributes, however, just two words sum up my experiences with him over the last 39 years . . . simply, thanks.'

Placid Gonzales

'Mike shows that he cares about you as a person and your family, and this creates incredible followship.'

Simon Monks

'I have worked for Mike for 40 years. He is a very special human being. He relates to people of all walks of life and makes them feel important.'

Myra Jones

'Mike has probably the best personal skills to deal with and motivate staff, advisers and clients that I have ever experienced or ever will experience.'

Trevor Downing

'From a personal point of view there is no one – and I mean no one – that has had a bigger influence on my business life.'

Tony Hannigan

'Mike's message is always to remember the journey, to give back to those less fortunate than yourself and act with compassion and humility.'

Steven McKnight

'Words cannot convey how special Mike is. He commands respect, admiration and loyalty from all who know him and is a natural born leader.'

Amina Kamal

'If you could bottle him it would make this country great again.'

Alan Pentelow

'As an ex-army officer, I have served under many great senior officers. Mike Wilson's leadership qualities top them all. He is, quite simply, the most inspiring person that I have known during my entire career.'

Richard Eaden

'Being involved with Mike completely changed my life and I am sure reading and acting on this book will change yours too.'

John Guthrie

'Mike has the constant ability to make YOU feel important, special, acknowledged and respected, and yet really all of those accolades belong to him. I respect him with such vigour and enthusiasm and so was thrilled and excited by the possibility that even some of his wisdom, achievements and kindness could be captured in a book. I am absolutely certain it will be a life gift to anyone who reads it.'

Gina Parker